TONALITY
IN COMMUNICATION FOR THE HOSPITALITY INDUSTRY

DR. SHARMADAS SENASI
(DBA), (MBA)

PARTRIDGE

ISBN:	Hardcover	978-1-5437-5926-6
	Softcover	978-1-5437-5924-2
	eBook	978-1-5437-5925-9

Print information available on the last page.

To order additional copies of this book, contact
Toll Free +65 3165 7531 (Singapore)
Toll Free +60 3 3099 4412 (Malaysia)
orders.singapore@partridgepublishing.com

www.partridgepublishing.com/singapore

CONTENTS

ACKNOWLEDGEMENT

I would like to thank the "International Business School of Scandinavia" for giving me the golden opportunity to participate and to complete my "Doctorate" program in Malaysia. Also, to the Lecturer whom has given me advice and guidance to create a benchmark for myself.

Nevertheless, to my parents whom has supported me through this book which I am publishing, guiding me through the knowledge on what they have experienced in life especially my father, whom has coached me and by explaining and defining things which would be easier for me to understand.

To all my group studies team, I do salute them for always keeping in touch with each other and having the liberty to meet up to discuss on our topic. Always keeping track with one and another ensuring we complete our research work and going through all ideas to mitigate flaws.

To all the Supervisors whom has bared with me all this time, I salute you for keeping us on track, ensuring we reach the level of our capabilities by which to provide the sufficient data which is collected and to put them at their designated place for the work we have completed.

PROBLEM STATEMENT

Disengagement in communication with differentiation tonality application failures.

STRATEGIES

To research and over view different ways of using "Tonalities" in communications by understanding its multivariate functions and methodology equation. This helps enable to mitigate communication problem and provide a linking pin of better understanding the concept of using "tonality" and the effectiveness.

To provide findings and justification that "tonality" does create a better bridge in the art of communication, where facial expression, para language and body language all are being used.

To create special techniques in training for the development of "tonalities" and "listening" to better understand communication, hence this mitigates miscommunication and improve self-development skills. Creating a questionnaire to be given out to actual trainees and getting feedback to generate graph and to collect actual data.

INTRODUCTION

In this "Dissertation", the writer would like to improve on the communication by using the right "tonality" to pass information and to communicate between the employees and customers, this will also assist in the mitigation of problem issues arises by the customers.

I would like to thanks to all the authors for their research for enabling me to research on the methodology of my "dissertation" and to come with an improved solution.

Communication is the most important and mostly been used in the hospitality & tourism industry, this will also determine on the tonality being used to exchange the frequency of information. It exists by both or more parties to exchange information amongst them self, such communication through tonality is not being spread well amongst all, this may cause a strain of burden for those who does not understand and will surely will cause a friction between all parties. (Ukessay.com- D'Annunzio-Green, Norma)

The hospitality industry is a very fast-paced industry where staff are not sitting down behind computers, yet they are communicating and entertaining guest every day without fail.

Customer expect fast and exceptional service for what they have paid for while staying or dining at your establishment, ensuring their service has been carried out with precision.

Communication is an exchange of words between people or more than 2 people, as when of which words are exchange, an understanding or instruction has been given. Imagine that a pilot has to land a plane and the communication between the pilot and the air traffic controller is not really clear, it will be impossible to understand the instruction and the pilot will not take any risk to land the plane when he is certain that the pilot gets a clear instruction without any mistake. (Study.com/Academy)

To have the experience of communication through the use of Tonality is very vital in any industry for any exchange of information in any sector e.g.: Hospitality, Hospital, Airports, Security and Police force and educational establishments.

In the hospitality industry, communication plays a major role in giving services to customers, imagine how would it be when the tonality of communication is not taken seriously, what will be the risk involve in any hospitality industry.

Any customers making any reservation will have a negative point of view in the establishment cause by wrongful use of communication and the tonality frequency.

The person who transmit informative communication, has to select the best possible way to pass information either through the use of email, fax, telephone, social media or verbal communication so the receiver may understand fully on what the intention of passing the information. The definition will be noted and understood by various ethnicity which will be visiting the establishment.

Communication failure do exist when the communicator does not transmit well to the receiver such as different ethnicity customers from various countries. This is main knows as "breakdown in communication" where the programming of the words is not match accurately for the receiver to understand, hence the tonality would have been adjusted to suited for customers with different ethnic background.

By transmitting fast pace tonality to a customer from France would be difficult, accent which they have develop along the years residing in France is greater accent which local Malaysian has, their hearing frequency is not been prepared for information which is being transmitted. The correct method would be to adjust our frequency in

order for them to follow through with our conversation by repeating it and asking them questions.
(Doug'o Brian-Blog)

Albert Mehrabian was the one who actually came up with a rule to determine about communication, the three important factors are "the word we use", "the tone we use" and "body language". (Taryn Davies)

KEY ELEMENT OF SUCCESSFUL COMMUNICATION

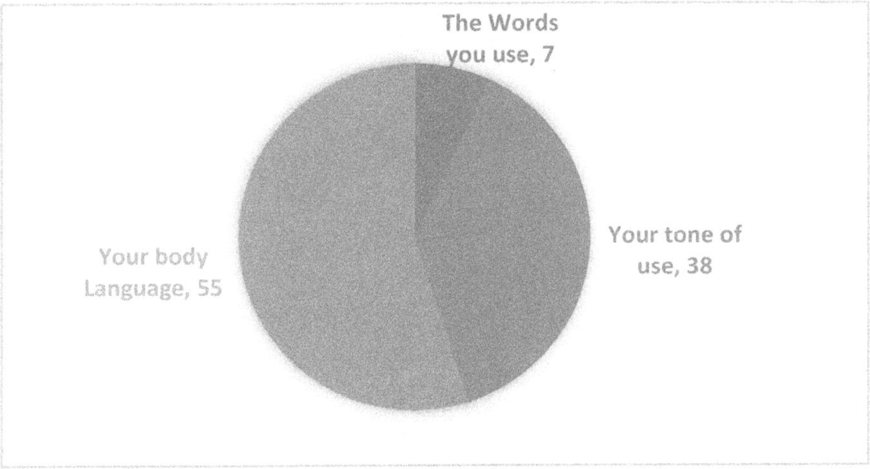

Consider speaking on the phone to our customers, they may not be able to see our body language hence the "tonality" of our voice depicts the expression of our core values and company values, it shows a lot more. To explain more about tonality, "Anthony Robbins" explain that understanding and practising (NLP) – ***"Neuro Linguistic Programming"*** enables us to better understand the way we communicate and use out tone in the proper order where we are able to justify many successful communication such as "business closure", "better discussion and understanding", "better relationship-Business or pleasure" and most important of all "better control of management leadership." (Anthony Robbins- Unlimited Power)

When using incorrect tone of voice, it can be very misleading, it develops instigation whereby hurt of feelings, cultivate arguments, thus can put off your customers choice of preference.
(Taryn Davies)

Daily experience in the hospitality has shown me many issues where staff has major issues in communication in Malaysia, proper screening has not been given hence speaking with a *"broken English"* which Malaysian's – terms used at Malaysia's; has cause many wrong interpretation amongst the customers and employees in the hospitality and tourism industry.

CHAPTER 1

Why is Tonality important in the Hospitality and Tourism Industry?

The word Tonality abbreviates through the art of proper communication and delivery process, tone give us the opportunity to market ourselves or creating a benchmark a position in business which define about a person and their capabilities. (Taryn Davies)

A consistent tone aids us to develop our very own branding which allows us to get the proper attention when delivering communications to our customers.

When communicating with passion or rough or angrily can have a great impact on how people interpret and look at you. Proper tone of voice may demonstrate a kind of warmth, happiness, excitement, and humour. Once the customer has won the heart and confidence of your customers, it will be easier to do potential business with them, promoting different business ventures or promoting your establishment in the hospitality industry. (Taryn Davies)

Communication also deals with the body language where we have developed over the years with all societies. Even a with a pleasant glance, eye contact and without saying a word may have a many meaning, people understand this method of facial expression which has been develop over the years without us knowing about it, this is known as emotion expression.

Linguist refers to all this auxiliary communication as paralanguage, this is important in tonality in communication which is been used. Paralanguage is widely been used while we communicate even in the phone, this can also be known as facial expression. (Dennis O'Neil)

When customers identify a comfort tone, they will picture a branding or the establishment, a personal benchmark where they have the confidence to listen and communicate with calm and ease. Their heart will have a kind of believe that what you say and what you deliver is services which is worth a thousand words. Customer do feel the comfort of being closer to you, the excitement of a customer always calling your name is where they have created a brand of uniqueness, hence marketing or promoting products and services is always to be agreed upon. Tonality develops the marketing part of us, by managing the way we communicate using the effectiveness of our tone will develop a strong relationship.

Imagine if a customer realises that we are communicating with a high frequency of tone and not having a proper body language such as putting your hand in both pockets creates a bad impression, the customer sense of loyalty will put in harm. The confidence of a customer which he had imagine, due to the structure and atmosphere of the establishment would have been corrupted due to the tonality and body language which was seen and experience would have given him a negative aspect towards the establishment. The customer whom has understands that the establishment representative as an "ambassador" is put to jeopardy due to the tonality and body language for first impression.

In communication, a speakers words are only a fraction of communication, there are several attributes which has to be considered in a proper communication which are the tone of your voice, the frequency of your voice which you are delivering to your listener, there is the body language which is the most vital and the fundamental of every communication.

"Dr Albert Mehrabian" rules of communication which actually define a break down percentage to communication. It is to believe that not only spoken words are important, yet the facial expression and body language plays an impeccable role and any conversation. It is to believe whenever we deliver our communication, we do not normally stand to a still, there is no way a person delivering important information will stand in still and communicate. By not properly utilizing our full body and facial movement, important clues pertaining to the information being delivered may have been wrongly interpreted by many listeners.

Professor Dr Albert Mehrabian and determine with his case study and research that words, Tone of voice and Body language is based on 7%, 38% and 55% of overall communication. In many articles I must strongly agree with several experience I have experience that standing alone without any body language and facial expression has been determine to not pass proper communication hence it caused lots of confusion in communication based such as conversation, training and marketing.

> ***"The non-verbal elements are particularly important for communicating feelings and attitude, especially when they are incongruent: if words and body language disagree, one tends to believe the body language."-*** *Prof. DR. Albert Mehrabian-http://www.rightattitudes.com/2008/10/04/7-38-55-rule-personal-communication/*

Feeling and attitude is the major player of communication, without this factor's listeners may process the wrong information because of inconsistence of the tonality of voice, facial expression and the emotion which to contemplate your discussion.

The three major elements to put into consideration in communication according to Mehrabian is that spoken words is 7%, tone of voice is 38% and body language is 55% must all be put together to structure your conversation in communicating with others.

If we choose the wrong words it is definitely going to trigger an ego of the listener which he will definitely will start an argumentative approach despite of listening properly before exchanging his words in a proper way. These three parts of the structure needs to support the message which is being converse by the speaker in order for the listener to understand and focus on the speaker. When the body language is not being utilised, many fraction of the communication will become meaningless, listener will presume that you are personally attacking him due to political conflict in the work place, this will cause distortion in the work place, what trust has been earn would have been destroyed due to in properly utilization with these 3 breakdowns of communications.

Variation of the tone of voice may vary when speaking to friends, business colleagues, our children's and to our loved ones, there are three breakdowns which we have to consider when having a proper communication.

Mood:

A person mood depicts the person when they are communicating, it is a sense of personal expression, and a good mood will have a very huge impact in making a business conversation and sealing the agreement. This also helps to deliver words to our loved one without causing misunderstanding. This can also be associated with "NLP" which the author of "Unlimited Power- Anthony Robbin" mention that if we program ourselves every day to be successful in whatever we are trying to do, the results will be a successful one due to our emotions which we have given a priority of be a better person. Positive emotion has a tremendous impact in our mind which gives us the confidence, a meaningful delivery of speech and creates a powerful approach by programming our self with positive thoughts. – (Anthony Robbins)

If the mood has a negative impact, this will cause a major negative impact towards our listeners, information which is rendered will cause many misunderstanding in defining the meaning of the communication.

Medium:

There are many segments of medium available when delivering a proper information which can relate to, this will include a written communication information where the use of social media will be an added advantage. Using a written communication information is a game changing plan, to ensure that proper message is being delivered where we have to ensure that the information is given is properly translated from speaking to written, ensuring that pictures for marketing is authentic and not fake and finally the information given is properly explain the purpose of the information. (Tom Albrighton)

Audience:

In this topic, choosing an audience with feasibility studies is very essential, demography studies have to be done to create which area to monopolise. For an example, if we are selling wedding services package then we have to identify wedding planners and young people ages from 20 till 45 years of age. Our brand needs to speak to people, information inserted has to relate to them and do not mislead them with other irrelevant information. (Tom Albrighton)

Communication in the hospitality is vitality important in every industry and organisation, this evolve human interaction through the use of human behaviours. Communication with proper tonalities is not an automatic method to be used, it takes practise and several training to improve its method to be a master user of "tonality". Once the art has been forged and crafted, it will be easier to communicate properly with different kinds of customers from any region part of the worlds.

The most common challenges when facing various types of customers are usually demanding when they are in a hurry, tired while travelling and feeling frustrated due to delays of transportation and transits. This also to be included that guest aspect to anticipate customers request and to deliver good service where ever and whenever is necessary. Hospitality staff needs to ensure their communication skills is impeccable due to the reviews given by other experience former customers through the use of "Trip Advisor" which has given many changes in the Hospitality Industry.

Many techniques are required to be obtain where many hospitality schools have yet to improve on the communication skills and method of executing to be an important tool in the hospitality industry. Methods need to be focus on are "Active Listening Skills", "Handling the telephone enquiry", "the intangibles" and "be prepared for situations". (Angella Ostroff)

Active Listening Skills:

Several exercises have been developed to improve listening skills, the way to hear a proper conversation is different than listening to a conversation. Is an added advantage to go thru specialize training which are mainly offered by various trainers, this is an "a training workshop" where is helps elevate and develop proper listening skills and coordination in the work place. An interesting site where research was done to improve on listening skills where is called "office oxygen" http://blog.trainerswarehouse.com/communication-exercises/

Where is provides many work shop to improve on listening skills, where such skills is developed by listening instruction by art of folding paper which is believe to coordinate your mind as to follow clear instruction given by the trainer. There are several trainings which has been develop to improve listening skills where this will definitely focus a positive respond through the art of games.

Relay the Message:

This exciting game, or known as "running dictation," is a fantastic game which activates an ice breaker, this is a natural introduction topic to understand each other and creating an awareness by listening.

The game plan:

To put students in pairs or groups of five, by assigning one or 2 students as runners and one to be assign as a writer to dictate. There will be messages written on a sticky paper where it is stuck on the other side of the wall. This will be exciting exercise where the student has to run and read the message as much as they can and to pass the message to the other students so they may continue with the communication and listening skills which is currently being develop by themselves. The aim is the development of these skills for the writer and reader to communicate which assist in development.

What does it take to communicate with another person, humans are contradicting that communication is merely a conversation and exchange of words? Does the effect of communication with the use of tonality really mitigates confusion? Communication and tonality are one segment where is defines as using the correct tone to communicate at the highest level of communicating. This defines as a logic, the art of tonality and para-language both representing each other to passively create an aptitude in branding and position oneself or achieve the highest level of communicating.

Improve Moods:

A study was done in the Year 2010 that smile can increase your moods and increases your positive element and thoughts. This magnificently reduces anxiety and improves the wellbeing of the person *"Quoted by Lt. Col (RTD) Datuk Dr Senasi Annamalai"- Consultant General Surgeon "Putra Specialist Hospital Melaka, Malaysia".*

"Smile" can be a non-verbal approach where the process of "NLP" is been programmed automatically making the body feels energetic and full of positive vibes.
Erin Coleman, R.D., L.D.**s**

Lowers Blood Pressure:

A 2009 review has shown that laughing actually relaxes your heart by increase of heart rate followed by a period of muscle relation which occurs in the body. As an interview with "Lt. Col (RTD) Datuk Dr Senasi Annamalai" mention that laughing releases a type of hormone known as "Endorphins" where give the human body a sense of excitement.

Stress Relieves:

When we are in stress, the body heart rate and blood pressure increase which due to high level of stress. When we often smile or laugh, these stress level reduces and gives a balance and alignment to our body. As a witness experience have seen many stresses personal often listen to music and tells listen to "YouTube" to find that comfort zone of calmness and relaxation, this may be for 15 minutes or less. A burst out laughs or smile has definitely assisted many in managing stress. (Erin Coleman, R.D., L.D.**s)**

Better Relationship:

Smiling a lot has brought many attentions to oneself, most of everyone gather to you due to your continuing of smile and laughter's, this is tangible evidence which is responsible to bring out the positive vibes out of your body.

According to "Lt. Col. (RTD) Datuk Dr. Senasi Annamalai", positive vibes or known as "The law of Attraction"- (Anthony Robbin) has gain many positive attributes due to the nature of smiling.

Stronger immune Function:

Smiling also has a special twist of ingredient where it boosts the immune system in the human bodies. (Dr Brit Phillips). Smile require 5 to 53 muscle in your body, but just by smiling only require your 5 muscles.

Pain Relief:

Helps to release its own naturel Pain killers through emotional response by the human brain. The benefit that the brains is capable of healing its self is remarkable. (Dr. Brit Phillips)

Smile and laughing actually increases your pain threshold.

Longer Life:

Smile intensify longevity and increase health. The more humans smile is likely to increase their life span but there is no accurate years on how long they will live.

Many whom are always joyful in life often life longer but the perception is always in the body and mind where positive thought and feeling boost enzymes that controls the aging factor of the body. (Michael L. Kruger)

Tonality in communication is also based on your personal personality, attitude, the way you are raised by your family, your culture and your heritage. The way a person speaks to their friends, loved ones and bosses are being used with different variation of tones and the choice of words used.

Languages used in conversation, sending text, syntax or email determine on the choice of words been used to communicate, customers often get offended on the choice of words used with the tone been put into the conversation. An example in conversation with a friend is when a very funny joke has been told, but the use of the wrong tonality is being used, the understanding of the joke is received by all receiver but there is no laughter's or smile just because the joke was told in a very lame way. Another example is when talking to your customers is always advisable to add humour to the conversation to emphasize their way of conversing, some customer likes an free and easy conversation but with fact, some would like serious conversation with only facts and no humour, understanding this junction will anticipate our every movements in communication and the use of tonality. (Abhiroop Basu)

Each communication we exchange must have a sense of purpose, the ability to understand and must have the ability to match with the interest of conversation, abilities of performance and hobbies of interest. The communication has to be precise and straight to the point, there is no short cut or "short talk", reason for mitigating unnecessary conversation. Is always important to concentrate on the way to pronounce the correct abbreviation of words, the way we pitch our tone and the volume which we are using to communicate. To ensure the correct and effective method of communication is being used, there are several important factors needed for considerations. The use of "Pitched" should be always mid-range and this is determined to the crowd we converse and the types of occasion which demands it such as presentation, business meeting, celebration speech and funeral speech. This are the clear evaluation needed to be considered to oneself when choosing a pitched for the delivery of speech.

The quality of the speech should be precise, should not be harsh, nasal or out of breath. This will expose the weakness of your speech and effect the branding you are developing for oneself. By not delivering a correct quality of speech will jeopardize the conversation which is been build and creating. A Perfect example is when speaking while having a bad "FLU" or "COUGH" this will definitely affect the pitch of your tone, the frequency you are trying to match and the correct para-language used which will affect the performance of a person ability.

Speaking with the correct "Rate" is very important, these medium rates of speaking acknowledged understanding by the receiver, when the rate is not been delivered with a stable tone it is likely our receiver will not understand or grasp the message that is been relayed. The correct method of using "pause" while communicating give the listener to listen properly and catch-up to what you are trying to deliver-hence the point of interest of understanding is achieved. Is also brilliant to avoid using the word "Haaa", "Ermmm", "Ahhh", "Umm" and "you know" which is not very professional in any conversation which effect the branding of the personality and company. In Malaysia, a very famous accent been used in all conversation which is the "Lah" word, a very annoying word but is being used constantly in Malaysia and Singapore which the origin of this word from the Chinese language, an "Asian Root-Slang" This choice of word is basically a culture imbedded with the Malaysia and Singapore heritage due to the Cultural heritage which has been obtain by many inter-cross marriages between so many cultures hence is a word which been used to obtain attention. (urbandictionary.com)

A very important way of communication is never to use "Jargon", the receiver may not understand the meaning due to their culture and educational preferences, hence this will cause many confusions in understanding the message which is been relayed.

CHAPTER 2

Communication in Tonality with different ethnicity

Many travellers have trouble with their second language or third language, the pronunciation will be very puzzling where words derived from their mouths are different and hard to understand. The difficult part is identifying their grammar and vocabulary which they used since their accent is strong with their mother tough language.

This usually occurs when they are in stress, when they are unable to communicate due to converting their mother tough language to "English" where the vocabulary used is totally unrecognisable. This will apply to those are using "English" which are from France, Germany, The Caribbean's where they often share the trade of cultural difference and a barrier between their language. (Rupert Goold - director of West End run of Oliver and multi-award-winning Macbeth)

Communication between different ethnicity is the vital part in influencing in major upselling products, this helps us to carefully control the use of our "tonality" in order to balance the accent which our customer has. For an example: A client from France will be speaking thru her strong French accent, but in order to deliver

information to her, careful use of voice by stretching of words and voice is very important in communicating. Thus, the use of body language, eye expression and simple sign language will eventually build the gap between bridges to easier to have a strong contemplation between both parties.
(Kara Brodie, Gary Abel)

Before the conversation has begun, many has the perception based on their race and age which causes a conclusion whether the understanding of what is being communicated is received properly without haste. (Rama Subramaniam, 2010)

Researching demographic of cultural and learning about different behaviour will not necessarily improve on cross-cultural communication, hence will only give you and inside of their heritage, how to approach them and to understand cultural believes. (Rossman, Marlene. L) -"Cross cultural communication"

The beginning of communication with a different culture, must be taken into consideration that the behaviour of the speaker such as punctuality, smile, personal space and humour may fail to improve due to cultural differences. Thus, ensuring to understand that cultural difference in communication has a huge impact with "miscommunication", often regards as being rude due to the frustration of delivering a message to the customers. (Rossman, Marlene. L) - "Cross cultural communication".

Many cultural differences try their best to assimilate what Malaysian hoteliers are trying to convey where the message gets distorted due to lack of correct information which is being used and the choice of words and para-languages.

Communicating with tonality with different ethnicity is a very challenging and needs to be research on how to improve the correct way of communicating, this also directs to the mater of difference in socioeconomic status, different in the speed of assimilation and difference in education.

Any business leaders or Hoteliers need to focus on their thought that intercultural knowledge is most of importance, it is also dealing with the expansion of globalization of the world and not to mention the work force which is being deal with various countries. The word cultures are defined as a set of values which many groups of people hold preciously, is the essence and heritage of their ancestors. These values effect the way we think, speak, feel and act which also assist us in judging other people around us. (Carol Kinsey Goman)

As humans, not everyone who belong to the same various types of culture, cultures are dynamic and changes through the life span.

Communication problems occur every time in every hospitality and business sector, this is due to the different of cultures and ethnicity which hospitality employee face when attending to their customers. There are three barriers to an effective multicultural communication which includes ***stereotyping, a lack of misunderstanding and judgemental attitudes.***
(Dr. Tyrone A. Holmes, Ed.D, LPC, CPT)

Stereotyping:

The most significantly habit which human beings has is the tendency to stereotype or most commonly known as ability to make assumptions on others which is based on an unidentified character such as age, religion, race, ethnicity, socioeconomic statues and their nationality. Most stereotypes always assume which cause a breakdown in communication wave, the assumption to see your customer and giving an unpredicted assumption about their life style and their attitude, this causes an irregularity when trying to communicate with them, a final conclusion which has been narrated wrongly due to gossips amongst the peers.
(Dr. Tyrone A. Holmes, Ed.D, LPC, CPT)

For an example that certain hospitality employees used to give an unpredicted or inconclusive evidence that just by looking at a customer's face and where they come from is actually not very friendly and does not tip well. Giving an incorrect information between their

peers on where the customers comes from. A flaw based on one's satisfaction to judge a person without speaking or uttering a word and their body language, often rumours are spread just to make a valid point so the employee whom gossips get attention. No matter which region of country, stereotypes who does not mitigate these types of occurrence will greatly diminish the art of communication effectiveness.
(Dr. Tyrone A. Holmes, Ed.D, LPC, CPT)

The lack of Understanding:

Understanding also depends one's background and status, managers understands difficulties compared to a clerk. The biggest problem in effectiveness of communication and lack of understanding is the failure to listen and understand, always presuming that the topic is just to understand but not able to justify the main criteria of the topic. Many people have different belief, values, ego, working styles, frequency to understand and personality types. The biggest problem of all with human being is that their mental "EGO" which they are highly proud of. In order to effectively understand communication exchange between their conversations, is the ability to understand their thoughts, feeling of idea, willing to contribute ideas or topic, styles, desire and emotions. The most important of all is the connectivity with the emotion while communication and understanding. Due to the communication partners, information is not being relayed properly and they take it for granted that their partners understand the message which they have relayed.

The most successful way of understanding and communicating with other is the ability to empathize or known as "put yourself in the other person shoes" to understand where they are coming from. Is always better to understand them at the beginning which will resolve the miscommunication and understanding. Unfortunately, in our fast-paced world which trending very vigorously is not taking the time to understand where they are coming from and what they

are actually trying to say, frustration builds up fast which causes the breakage in understanding.
(Dr. Tyrone A. Holmes, Ed.D, LPC, CPT)

Judgemental attitudes:

The judgemental expression and contradicting are the most major factor in effective cross-cultural communication when we are interacting with many other people. These is the main essence of ethnocentrism, the process where we evaluate the good and the bad, the right and the wrong. To effectively interactive communication whom are different to us, it is advisable to suspend all judgemental attitudes aside and try to understand them from their perspectives.
(Dr. Tyrone A. Holmes, Ed.D, LPC, CPT)

These are the three significant barriers which has the capability to disrupt proper communication and to share point of views in a profession way. To eliminate these barriers, there are 3 strong steps to take into consideration to improve your conversation skills, communications and tonality.

These barriers are to ***enhance your self-awareness, increasing your empathy and suspending judgemental***. By using these following steps, it shall mitigate or remove the three significant barriers which caused confusion and problem for conversing.

Enhance your self-awareness:

It is advisable to understand those whom are stereotype and to ensure to mitigate the impact on your conversation, the communication which you have with others may have an impact on the cultural differences. It has to be understood that stereotypes is an unconscious process which may severely effects the communication skills and what it is being delivered to. This unconscious process

always appears when having to defend something which normally cultivates a person "Ego" when in questioned, where the process of stereotypes always to make an assumption without prove of evidence or facts. The self-awareness is the tendency to managing to control emotion, attitude and behaviours, hence to have the awareness to mitigate errors not to be emotional while having a conversation. Self-preservation of respect is mostly an importance to develop self-control. The other way of control emotion and strengthen to enhance your self-awareness is to attend qualifies counselling which allows you to control those emotion and put it into a perspective way of communication. A speech therapist is also an example of improving one's self.
(Dr. Tyrone A. Holmes, Ed.D, LPC, CPT)
(Benbassat, Jochanan MD; Baumal, Reuben MD)

Increasing your empathy:

The word empathy is defined as putting yourself in one's shoe and seeing from his perspective which allows you to understand more from his point of view. If you understand the word empathy, it is the single most important word to understand in multi-cultural communication and the usage of tonality. To understand empathy, one's must understand multi-cultural and their heritage, allow one's self on the journey to understand by having a deep conversation about their back ground, culture and habits. Listening to their life style also plays major role in increasing your empathy. By attending to cultural society and cultural events will broaden your knowledge with multi-cultural difference and communication, which is one of the best way in increasing your empathy level. Another way of also improving is attending cultural organization which allows you to freely research your method of understanding and observing ways of communication and their para-language skills.
(Dr. Tyrone A. Holmes, Ed.D, LPC, CPT)
(Benbassat, Jochanan MD; Baumal, Reuben MD)

Bias Judgement:

The last conclusion we ought to tell our self is to stop judging people the way we look at them, how they walk and the way their life style is. It is very difficult for us to stop judging people because we have been doing it ever since, how we appraise people and evaluate people is also part of judging but is a more professional term to be used in the Hospitality and Business world. How we look at life and the way we asses our values, beliefs of individual and others is known as ethnocentrism, we must have the willingness to listen to people whether they may be right or wrong, is the basis of giving them a privilege to express them self.
(Dr. Tyrone A. Holmes, Ed.D, LPC, CPT)
(Benbassat, Jochanan MD; Baumal, Reuben MD)

The tonality and frequency of Tone Pitch:

The mechanics of our speech production is determining on the acoustic vibration which produced by vocal fold, which enable our muscle to interact with out vocal cords hence manifest into pitch tone of voice or taker's fundamental frequency. In the tone language, pitch of tonality abbreviated the definition of each words pertaining to its meaning. Tones are basically described as the relation of the talker pithing their voice to enable a frequency where the receiver understands hence does not disrupt the receivers EGO with over frequency pitch tones. For an example, the word in Tamil=Amma, when be raised the tonality is brings a rudeness when calling, hence when pitching high frequency enables the mother to know that she is been summon urgently. Also, in calling the word Amma in Tamil using a moderate tonality pitch frequency enables a loveable bond of connection. This also applies to Chinese speakers due to their high pitch volume. Patrick C. M. Wong, Ph.D., CCC-SLP, [1, 2, 3] Tyler K. Perrachione, M.A., [1, 4] Geshri Gunasekera, [1] and Bharath Chandrasekaran, Ph.D.[1]

The perception of a pitch is a very useful behaviour for understanding human behaviours, certain pitch gives an emotional distress to the receiver. An example by pitching high frequency and by scolding an employee will change the perception of the employee hence demotivating them while working. If gentle tone or pitch is use to advise them, it will be a very new ball game where the employee will feel more motivated and eager to learn more but will try to mitigate mistakes. Patrick C. M. Wong, Ph.D., CCC-SLP, [1, 2, 3] Tyler K. Perrachione, M.A., [1, 4] Geshri Gunasekera, [1] and Bharath Chandrasekaran, Ph.D.[1]

In many communications that we observed, there are three most important words we should know, the "3V's" which we must consider before participating in any communication whether social or professional, the 3V's is "Visual, Vocal and Verbal". The 3V's play an amazing role in charactering a person intension for communicating, listening to different accent may lead to the use of the 3V's where we visualize the person communicating with use and understand their tonality. Hence to listen to their vocal communication carefully to see their lips on what they are trying to say, and last but not least and the verbal interaction we have with them which make it a smooth sail.

The three V's is actually a valuable tool where it will be widely used as to improve customer service and increase profitably in the hospitality industry. Such influence can generate a sense of satisfaction following "Anthony Robbins" the book he wrote called "Unlimited Power".
(Anthony Robbins- Unlimited Power)

In the events of an actual communication, the actual message which is being transmitted through our vocal will effect and influence by vocal tone and body language. A different body language will influence the message on what we are trying to say, this will definitely impose a question mark for the opposite direction or towards our employees and customers. A simple tonality which depict sarcasm can eventually change the whole sentence differently which would influence the definition differently. Adding a visual component such as rolling of eyes, nodding of head or shoulders will define the sentence to another definition where it would be misunderstood by many. Patrick C. M. Wong, Ph.D., CCC-SLP, [1,2,3] Tyler K. Perrachione, M.A., [1,4] Geshri Gunasekera, [1] and Bharath Chandrasekaran, Ph.D.[1]

CHAPTER 3

Improvement of Customer satisfaction and Profitability in the Hospitality Industry

The word communication is like a glue that keeps your customers intact and satisfied, these verbal interaction manages your ability to get their attention, their focus onto you, their interest of conversation, their ability to interact with you, their excitement which been boosted by your branding image and your tonality which keeps them intact like a glue. Communication is part of an organization that's builds you to become a better team player, it also creates a branding for yourself. Every hard work of communication creates a better result for your career baseline, a jump ahead to upsell your products and services. To improve on the customer's satisfaction, communication is not the only player, it should be a team player with the use of your verbal attributes, body language and most important of all is the tonality of using those language which will give you an ultimate power on giving the best customer satisfaction possible.

A good communication is not only using what we have learn over the year from our parents with good respectful skills such as "Thank you", "Yes Ma'am" "Please" and "I would be happy to", it also starts

with the understanding of "Phycology" on how to deliver the correct message to your customers or employees, the ability to always ask the right correct question and to answer them correctly and also to deescalate any anger or emotion which will affect the quality of your communications. Delivering a communication with the use of proper tonality, it is very important to focus on the question and answer with a position emotion and not allowing negative emotion to entangle your conversation.
(Adam Toporek- Author/ "Be your customer's Hero"-)

Maximizing customer satisfaction does indeed improve on profitability in any organisation especially in the Hospitality, increasing the profitability actually does assist many ways for continues repeat customers and generate more revenue for the company. This also allows us to control on marketing budget where putting endless effort in customer satisfaction with the use of proper communication, tonality and para-languages. Satisfied customers always do recommend new client to your establishment hence the marketing tool of word by mouth is created as a self-awareness tool. (Ian Linton)

Many customers and business people usually takes their recreation or business elsewhere due to the insufficiency of customer care in communication and human interaction due to several weaknesses in the company training method. Such meticulous training should be considered to win the hearts of the customers, branding will be in severe jeopardy due to untrained and unprofessional staffing. Most common of all is the effects of revenue income for the company where customer began to realise that there is a severe issue on customer service and communication within the company and customers, a tragedy yet to be affected.

To suggest a consultant company specializes in Communication through tonality will be the most ideology preference for the company to engage with, hence will improve on customer satisfaction. No matter what scale size of the business, it is proper to see the customer as an independent conscious individual deciding where to spend their money. Hiring knowledgeable personal is one of the advantages to ensure your customers are being dealt with appropriately. Customers do feel satisfied when they are able to speak to an educated and trained personal, which makes the conversation very informative, this gives them the purpose to re-visit your establishment just to be served again. (Mitchell Holt)

Customers do feel relax when the customer service personal speak to them through the phone with a tonality which can be related as polite, humble and knowing the product knowledge. This enable them to have a positive view on the services rendered and about the business property management. Telemarketing also plays a very important role in selling products and services, hence by putting the right individual employee with a proper training equal the continuation mass sales increase. Any part of communication with the use of tonality, for an example by using the telephone, plays an important image and role, not thinking as micro marketing but thinking as macro marketing is to understand the target audience we are looking for. Looking at demographic and to monopolize your audience is to ensure that your customers service through communication and tonality plays a serious role in getting your audience interest and making them as your stake's holders. (Mitchell Holt), (Anthony Robbins).

Customer also do feel excited when every one of the employees knows their products and how to create their personal branding, human rights are a big concern when comes to all customers feeling satisfied to see the employees are happy and well treated. The communication and tonality given to the employee has to ensure that employees are taken care very well, such as medical benefits and other tricks and perks do enable the employee to stay longer and be sincere with the establishments. There is a metaphor in the hospitality that the customers do follows the employee serving them, making them as a personal butler for their comfort, many occasion has resulted that customer who usually visit the establishment always calls their favourite waiter, waitress or supervisor because of the communication between them, hence the service provided to them. (Mitchell Holt), (Anthony Robbins).

According to the University of Maryland's "Robert H. Smith" school of business, mentioned that a good customer service can measure or manoeuvre customers point of view, by using the proper tonality of voice, special and powerful representative of words will measure their interest to change their mind set and to follow an advice what the customer service has to offer; this probably can be called at "NLP". (Nicole Long)

In profiteering area, customer's feedback is vitality important in getting different product knowledge from other competition which gives a benchmark on your competitor on how to sell different product with using the information given by the customers. This information is most vital in improving the communication and tonality to improve customer's feedback experience and their product interest measure. The department of customer's service does understand the nature of greeting, treating and handling of customers product and services, this gives the comfort that if any problem were to occur, the customer service is enabled to solve the problem from occurring. This area of concerns represents the profit which the company will be benefiting due to the ways of customers service is been provided, hence benefiting with the repeat customers providing support every step of the way. (Nicole Long)

Loyalty is one of the most importance in securing customers with their confidence, this also do effect on the profiteering mechanism where once again touching on the getting, solving problems efficiently and quick, mitigating problematic events and ensuring positive results to the customers all do give a good impression to the customers to stay loyalty, to be cautions not to break their promises ones it has been given will tremendously create a conflict between the customer and the company. In motion, a very happy customer's do create a positive vibes and happiness where the spreading of marketing and advertising is in effect immediately, now with social medias is been marketed instantly with the use of "Facebook", "Instagram", "WhatsApp" and many other social media applications. The use of word of mouth is constantly been marketing and advertise for you and there is no cost or charges to the company, branding is created and self-awareness is built by the customers happiness and confident is gained by others. Improvement of sales and the measurement of the profitability will increase due to proper customers care services rendered, proper tonality and communication skills been spoken in the hospitality industry, where this will be great for other businesses to achieve the same standard.

In an organization, the organization staff is the biggest expense in investment but buy putting the investment at the correct place and pace, it can generate a better yield and profitability due to the excellence of communication skills. Some communication goes beyond outside of the world, most of it occurs internally between the employees and management. There is a flaw in their communication due to insufficient training been provided or the wrong types of people giving the training which has been contemplating between the two work teams that leads to severe breakdown in communication where the tonality does not comprehend any dialogues. Organization needs to focus and invest in their employees to find a suitable training for their team so they may improve the art of communication, many organizations hired or outsource training team which specially deals with communication ethics. This is not only about language but is the way the information is been delivered and been passed down accurately and precise.
(Telephone Doctor-service skills-st.lois)

Companies often like to retain their employees with benefits to string them down so they will not leave, they fail to see that this method is useless without adequate training such as language command, communication skills and do not give them any competitive edge on promoting themselves climbing the ladder in becoming an executive. Companies or hotels after see the "ROI" return of investment which fails the profitability in improving customer experience through the right employees entertaining the customers and making their joyful occasion a fruitful one. Company who invest on employee's communication not only benefit by improving their self-awareness and skills, they even improve the customers experience, these brings in customers satisfaction where promotion of word of mouth is instantly been marketed and other customers begins to visit the establishments. (Telephone Doctor-service skills-st.lois)

Human Behaviour effecting the Tonality in Marketing?

An effective marketing produces results, satisfaction, teamwork and revenue for any industry, the vibration of tonality is very important which relates to phycology in human behaviours. The main goal is to promote a brand, product and information to various channels and to create a "linking-pin" so that channelling it will be easier, making sure the demographic or target markets gets the information. "Linking-pin" is define as a main base or an operation centre where the project consultants and employee may benefit will all obtainable resources needed in ensuring the smooth sail of the project market structures. In locating the right tonality for your brand of products will help foster loyal customers in purchasing your products, allowing them to experience the serenity, the luxury and the taste of lifestyle. (Vicky A. Benge)

The customers experiencing the branding of the product eventually starts with their own tonality structure coordinating wisely with friends and family in marketing the product, services and branding they have witness and experience. A simple marketing structure which gossip at the ears of new potential new customers which will eventually spread more marketing efforts to others of their contacts. Tonality can be varied through youthful, enjoyment and securing important resources where can be used for the future in obtaining credibility in ensuring that's the product and branding is strong. The message which is intended to be passed on can be in a playful manner, cautious manner or even in a serious and professional manner. (Vicky A. Benge)

Having your target audience plays an important role in producing results and revenue for your company, this heightens your rating where branding is involves. A strategic plan to choose your target audience makes it a strategies way to formulate your message following with the correct tonality to be used to reach your audience, the tonality may vary with the different target audience such as age, culture, life styles and professionalism. (Vicky A. Benge)

The art of communication engages in our intellect, sense of emotions and also stimulate our senses which finally goes to embracing your spirit. Hence this also allows us to create our branding of our personality and creates character which allows us to mingle with many types of people. Many communication metaphors resonance and some also leave us dissonance, even yet it also energised us and some will eventually leave us depleted. We always talk to our colleagues, children, friends and family but how often do we realise that we are communicating effectively without us knowing, hence interacting effectively needs to develop trust and understanding what are your goals in order to effectively use your tone to communicate.

When a human is feeling scared, defensive or nervous it is likely the tonality of the person voice will automatically change without her knowing, this is caused due to emotional distress where the ripple effect effects the tone causing a action and a reaction. (Judy Jablon 2015)

Tonality varies from cold to warm, critical to supportive and authority to collaboration, it connect to every path available and this create emotion where it also stimulates reasons and purpose. In every action there is a counter reaction where the tone of your voice creates an awareness and also created a judgement by others, by using it to the fullest we have to carefully choose the correct word, phrase, verbs and tone to deliver what we are intending to say. Our tone explains who the person is by emphasis on certain words, body language and facial expression which contributes to para-language which eventually conveys our attitudes whether we send our message of humour, jealous, sarcasm, anger or sad. (Judy Jablon 2015)

What does it take to communicate with another person, how do we communicate with a person without using any words which is called non-verbal language and we have been using it every day without us knowing about it? Albert Mehrabian's work on non- verbal and verbal communication in the year 1960's and 1970's has been considered a very valid model today, thank to him we have improved on it which gives us the meaning to communicate. He has also found out that many people believe more on the non-verbal communication then the verbal communication itself. On the other hand, the same sentences can have multiple meaning and definition, for an example ***"Are you telling me the real story"*** this sentences is a direct sentence but this also have another meaning which reveal another agenda such as ***"I don't trust you"*** or ***"I know you are lying***". Many people have the intention to create many anomalies just to satisfy their curiosity. (MTDTraining-Bookboonblog)

To understand the art of communication, one has to learn the concept of organizational behaviour, the phycology of human interaction, their emotions, their attitudes and their interactions amongst themselves. Organization behaviour main focus and study of human behaviour on their impact on the organisation within their group to which can be model to give a positive together with communication. A successful business is always dependant on the effectiveness management of its people and how they are taken care of. A successful team always develop better and always strive to perform the best of their abilities. Behaviours of people is always leading to their ideas, feelings and their activities. Their emotion normally triggers their behaviour where ego such as defensive habits, proud speaking, and high pitch tone are always seen while communication which eventually loses prospect due to unsatisfied customers. (Ashim Gupta-24/4/2010)

Since human behaviour can be change with different types of people, it is impossible to find the exact solution for their organisation, which is why it is very important to create solution based on phycology and social aspect to create a valid solution. The behaviour of a certain individual in any organization can either defile the company strategy

and destroy their team strength or assist them in maintaining a strong team in promoting product and services.
(Bhaswatti Bhattacharyya)

Certain employees who no longer trust their management or unsatisfied may have an antisocial reaction towards the management and their team, this will bring of a negative effect toward the team and with effect other employee in the process. Organization behaviour values are kept in a parameter of its values such as believe, trust, honesty, principles and it's believed. All of this effect may have a great positive impact towards our employee leaving them satisfies and happy causing a positive reaction and high impact on their performance. Employees are highly adaptive to their work cultures as long as the management correspond with their needs such as benefits, training, motivation and family outing which brings a special relationship with employee's family and management bonding, giving them an opportunity for the family to experience the management ethics and relationship towards their employees. The most important a management company should have and implement is a pro-social culture and a supportive management where is one of the most major influence is gaining confidence and morality from the employees hence developing confidence between internal employees and build an awareness of selflessness. When employees are encouraged with such confidence they begin to contribute to the company with ideas, time and effort which eventually leads to organization benefit would increase. (Bhaswatti Bhattacharyya)

Solving organization problem and to mitigate them from reoccurring is to first find the problem which is constantly occurring and try to evaluate the situation by analysing the problem such as where, when, why, what and how it is occurring. By managing these questions and answering them is likely that the management has the ability to get the answer they are looking for. It is important to recognise the behaviour problem and to ensure it can be identifying early and to be isolated within the company and treated at such to ensure the company employees will not be affected with this negativity. It is very encouraging to incorporate new and constructive behaviours in the organization which allows the employees to experience new ways of improving their self and to sustain the vulnerability to success such as personal achievements, encouragement and affiliations. The management should also find the solution to stimulate the drive of the employees in orders to maintain their motivation and perseverance. This plan can be the type of rewards, improvements of benefits, holidays or salary increments, employees often lose interest when the management does not acknowledge them or recognise them on what they have contributed for the success of the company. (Bhaswatti Bhattacharyya)

Organization behaviour is mainly related to social science where the study of human interaction and their sociology is measured to their performance and contribution. Logically it takes into account that behaviour and attitude which impacts on these performances and the behaviour patent seems to cause emotional reoccurrences which will affect the company performances. It is also necessary to understand the measure how these behavioural patent works on a company and how it takes into effect to manage it in the company. In many cases if the management can interpret the human needs and to plan and evaluate their strategy to plan and increase new performance level, benefits and career enhancement, it is surely to know that the benefits of the employees will be rewarding and satisfied. Such benefits and career enhancement plan may result to improvements within the management and employee. The management also needs to identify problematic employees and how to resolve the situation swiftly to ensure mitigation of these problem can be resolve permanently. (Bhaswatti Bhattacharyya)

CHAPTER 3

The Body Language

Humans do not need to reply on indirect messages like dog wagging its tail asking for food because we know when they feel hungry and when is time for walkies, hence human has an advance language capability and can state their desire very much clearly. In other words, body language is more highly develop in human because they have the most expressive face which tell a thousand words which developed in connection with a preferred front on interaction. There are powerful signs which are transmitted through the facial expression and human has a highly developed mind reading capabilities when someone is using their body language. This tool is highly used to determine or having a second guest when somebody has something in mind for us to validate their tones and facial expression. Mind reading abilities has been mostly retain by humans and evolved during the years which are considered a survival mechanism, these abilities has many aspects of telling us information what we cannot understand but what we can see and feel.

Body language does leak emotional information and attitude where we preferred to conceal it from other but other surrounding you may know it already, it is like the game "Poker" everyone always say to hold your "Poker face" straight meaning do not leak any emotional information through the facial expression. (Glenn Wilson-Body language)

What is the origin of a non-verbal code to which we are all responsive to it, the man behind this is the great evolutionist biologist "Charles Darwin" where he has pointed out that the expression of an emotion is actually been achieved by simply delivering a sample of residue or in a scientific term which is "Overt Instinctive Behavioural pattern". Just for an example we look at the work "Disgust" which literally means rejecting something, hence in out facial expression seems to be more on foul tasting which needs to be thrown out. The word fear also indicates its meaning in various ways such as by freezing, preparing to flee or holding someone for support. In one interpretation suggest the appearance of universal behavioural pattern of this type maybe taken into account as their instinctual origin.
(Glenn Wilson-Body language)

Majority of people capacity for reading body language is spontaneous at a certain age and some may be a slow process but the mind reading ability will be grown as maturity increase for humans. Let us look at posture and gesture where there is a definition to be made between posture and gesture, which is crucial in the body language. A gesture is a learned signal which involved only one part of the body which is usually the hand, where it intends to be disconnected from the rest of the body. When a person asked an individual for a street direction, that individual will only use his hands to point the direction but the rest of the body does not follow nor get involved. Gestural codes vary from different countries and continent, making a small circle between the forefingers and thumb has many different meanings and some does miscommunicate its meaning. We are very well known when making a circle with our fingers does mean "zero" or worthless but in Japan it defines as money but in Italy it has a different meaning to it which means homosexual. Different gesture has many significant meanings where it brings different definition to understand body language.

As to posture, this involved the whole body to act in concert, this usually invest greatly in greater emotional significant and does convey a deeper feeling. As before in gesture pointing a finger where only the hands move, just imagine when a child is about to get hit by a bus, our whole body moves with a vigorous emotional vibe which alerts many people surrounding us. Our body is getting align and to communicate the urgency of the situation where a phenomenal emotion going through the body, this shows the consistent, attitude, instinctive rather than an empty signal. The art of ready body language is to look past at gesture and evaluate posture to get a better understanding and the meaning of body language. (Glenn Wilson-Body language)

We often in many occasions always judge a book by its cover where many hoteliers often do this as a short talk where they immediate judge a person by their looks and by the way they talk, their body language and yet they sum up an immediate conclusion. It is like we are taking an immediate snapshot of a person and determines our reaction towards them. A person may change their point of view and regret what they have said about that particular individual once the person has spoken, how we see them speaking and how we find their remarkable personality to be humble with their virtues.

When people are being shown photograph of strangers faces where their personality has been assessed previously, people are able to detect an immediate response those who are high in "Psychotics"". This is actually a very major personality trait that is partly inherited and goes slightly weird in behaviour, irresponsibility, risk-taking, criminal activity and delinquency. However, there are a clear survival advantages in actually identifying and spotting someone whom are trust worthy, especially for a woman to choose her partner. (Glenn Wilson-Body language)

Primates spends more time face to face contact with each other and human do so as well, is part of their lifestyle, culture and a sense of belonging to see a facial expression which triggers an emotional feeling. This are the main reason why the muscles of our face are so highly developed as a signal for expressing feelings and attitudes. Example, smiling is one of the clearest and safest body languages which means friendly intend, Californian Psychologist "Dr Paul Ekman believes it is possible to create 7,000 different type of pattern of the facial muscle which is having its own shade of meaning.

Faces are highly expressive but they can also be very deceptive and also very difficult to read. This is because people themselves are in a conflict about how they should be reacting hence their mix feeling are the results of ambiguous signals. Faces is hard to read due to humans are complex social animals that have learn the art to suppress and to display their emotion for various reason. Human also like wearing a mask to hide their expression feeling, wearing a mask is not literally meaning wearing a mask hence to hide their feeling and emotion so others may not see what they are feeling.

As per women, their facial expression is easier to read due to their burst of emotional signals which blast it ways throughout their body and finger tips. Understanding women body language is not difficult, tasting a sour fruit may have well explode their taste buds and emotion to spread on to everywhere cause a chain reaction of ambiguous signals. This is because women are more to be more emotional expressive, their emotional is difficult to control where they have to find an output for it to be expelled out.
(Glenn Wilson-Body language)

The most vital thing to know about a person is whether do they like us or not, because this will determine the future of the on-going relationship which is wisely taken into an importance where staff and customers have to have a very good relationship due to the nature of future business contacts and its potentials. They are also some certain ritual like a special handshake gestures, greetings and gift which explain or give us a clue on how we regard them as. This clue is most important for us to identify their body language which gives us an advantage to identify their relationship.

Mirroring can be define as acknowledging a person with their same style of greeting, reflecting the body language is a very powerful tool of another person where it can be very interesting which indicate warmth because it can be deliberately manipulated to make another person feel comfortable and how we greet them. This make them feel comfortable with you that we make them feel welcome, such as meeting a client and asking them where they are from, the client responded by saying they are from France. So as a hospitality staff, they should understand how to greet in "French" such as ***"Bonjour, Como Cava", Je m'appelle Mr. Sharma-*** meaning "***Good day, how are you, my name is Mr Sharma"***. This ease the tension between customer's relation with the client where the client feels greeted well with their own language hence breaking the ice bearer which starts a whole new relationship between the hotel staff and customers. (Glenn Wilson-Body language)

In this current modern world is a fast paced and is also involved lots to deal with stress, communication has been advanced that we are efficiently on the call "24/7" even though we are supposing to be on holidays. Where ever we go in our careers, communication is the most important tools in the world, it has become prominent with different language with several different dialect, also with several different sign language.

The world as we know it, depend totally only communication such as direct or confrontational conversation, telecommunication and social media. The internet as we know it today has evolved dramatically where communication is being used daily, every minute and every second, the mass communication as we know it "Macro" marketing is being achieve everywhere.

Without communication at the work place or in general, none of the vital information gets passed on or even get process through our brain, hence leaving us in the "cold" meaning alone. Communication has now become an art, a dominant activity which is desired to be socialize and idealized, so imagine people in the hospitality industry where there is no communication, a catastrophe incident will happen which would shake the hotel industry by storm.

Communication is now been treated as art or other may call it as dancing with words, wisdom is created, theory is challenged and arguments are exchange, with all this the human body is still capable of seeing the hidden language, which is the body language. Everyone is advised to learn it and experience the art of reading body language, seeing a couple get together and smiling with each other tell a million story all together. Researchers, authors and professors now rely more than communication, they also rely on the wide use of social Medias as a channel for discussion and also the use on the internet.

Hospitality Industry is now having issues such as communication where the lacking of communication has been re-occurring, communication between lower management staff and entry level has all been affected, many of them think is only a business transaction they will have to look after but yet they are wrong. In the hospitality industry, communication is vital even to entry level position, this actually keeps everyone in place and makes them feel special. Working in the hospitality industry for many years has brought to many conclusions what can be done to help improve the art of communication and to mitigate problems and issue internally and externally. None of the management employees has any idea that their communication and ego is destroying the hospitality industry not on financial level but in the human capital way, many employees strive to be the best but never has been acknowledge by the management even though they are entry level and have been working for the company for years. It is clearly a mistake why are the entry level are kept aside, that they are just a lower paid income earner which does not need respect, and they have been treated and given respect lower than other.

So, what is keeping them from respecting them and appreciating the work they have been doing for the company, the answer is clearly simple where management wears a suite and entry position just wears a simple uniform. The simple of things which make a huge difference, the ego of managements assuming that a suite bring them a higher power but we have to have a clear understanding, without the suite and the ego the business still goes on. The most important human capital is the entry level and the higher management which is the main mechanism in managing a Hotel, yet many believe that is due to how the upper management manages the property.

Do Body Language work on Upselling for profitability?

As for Body Language, the meaning varies from zone to zone and insource culture and countries, a gesture is acceptable while in other zone if is bad, it is difficult to understand adult's facial expression as they often hide because of social status.

Does body language do help in upselling product for the benefit of the property where revenue increases, the answer will be truly be "yes". With the combine effort of using the proper tonality frequency, proper language skills and a proper body language will be able to upsell many things to the customers. Customer loves pampering and they like to be amused, with this special concoction is will be a positive feedback for customer to say.

So why body language is so very important for the use in the hospitality and in any industry and why it is a must to be incorporated into a system. The actual fact and logic is that when every body language is been used by adopting many emotion a person has, it creates a special character where it calms many people down, they understand you and what you are trying to sell. They feel confident and their imagination starts to be creative with words and emotion what you are trying to deliver. Lastly, they feel they must try the product you are selling because they are feeling over whelm with the positive vibration which you are delivering. Never forgetting that we must understand what we are selling and understand the product knowledge well, we have to identify their positive and negative traits such as food where we understand how the taste buds works. What type of flavours exploding in our mouth and how is the sweet taste, the sour taste, the spicy taste and the texture all of this we have to experience before upselling to our customers?

It is a very good idea for new products to be sampled by the staff so they know what product they are selling, identification of a target market is necessary is vital and understanding the emotion which come from within our body that connect to our brains has a different sensation all together. Different individual has a different emotional response where someone love eating sweet delicacies may indulge with an emotion of love and serenity but a person who don't really like to eat sweet may have a different emotional expression such as their face and posture changes dramatically showing that the food is too sweet.

Body language as we speak it every day consist of certain pattern, when we observe them carefully it tells a thousand story of that emotion and even to describe it further each body language has its own sentence, introduction, thriller, synopsis, conclusion and ending. Body language is best described as "dancing of the soul" where it is believed that the body has plenty to share and thousands of impulse and chemistry is passing through the nerve and veins.

Here is a scenario, having an oven fresh hot "lasagne" to be sold in the coffee house of a hotel restaurant, is the job of the waiter and their teams to upsell the delicious oven cooked hot lasagne to their customers. The question arise is how will they upsell this magnificent dish and to create a branding.

After several session of brain mapping experience, there is a way to sell the "Lasagne", first of all is to choose it "Branding name" a name where is special and attracts attention by everyone. The branding name has to associate with their countries season such as "spring", "autumn", "winter", and "summer" and let's say it is summer and what has summer has to offer. The main plan is to choose a suitable name of the "Lasagne" where is has to do with "summer". Having a name just "Lasagne" is totally old school but having a twist on its name will have opposite chain reaction by the customers, a name which "Brands" itself with "Dignity", "Lavish", "Rich" and "Flavour". Imagine using the name Lasagne but to amplify the name becoming **"Lasagne, flavours of summer"** and the description will be **"Summer red tomatoes and vegetables cooked in**

wild herbs served in a blanket of summer wheat with wild olive oil".

Decoration of the lasagne will be important where herbs are toss it to create a gastro experience, a branding by itself, an Oscar award nominee which tells itself is the most succulent taste of all. Branding is a positive way of introducing a new product hence the smell of the lasagne has to be smelled by everyone. Cooking in the kitchen will supress the smell of the lasagne but cooking in front of the coffee house where the smell erupts every taste bud and ignites all appetite.

The most important of all is to allow all the employee to taste the "Lasagne" so they may indulge on their own adventure and experience the taste of a perfect branding for the promotional season. NLP is not only while communicating, hence it can be used in words such as menu, programming a taste buds together creating a memorable experience while reading the menu create a hunger for taste.

Once the employee has tasted the "Lasagne", is now their turn to experience their journey of emotions and allow their body language to work its way out of their body and through their nerve and veins allowing them to explode their own branding of body language.

Once the smell of the lasagne has been implanted in the coffee house, many customers will wonder what that sensational smell is and would like to know what is that special meals that deserve an award by the customers. Hence the birth of a new body language and branding is born where applying the impossible to be possible.

Having a good presentation while communication has its advantages in giving an opinion to others while communicating with them. A good presentation orientates a person perspective such as their behavioural pattern, their focus, their listening skills and their attention. All of this is considered while wearing a full 3-piece suits, it explains a person aptitude and their committeemen to communicate with a function to impress and give meaning to a customer's stay.

The cloths we wear and how it changes us:

It is very logical that a behavioural pattern depicts a person way of dressing up with various style, a person with a 3 piece suite may have a different behavioural pattern then a person wearing a uniform to work, and it is how the attire that we wear creates a different personality all together. Clothing has a very large impact on our inter-personal skills, at such it creates our way of speaking, our way of walking and the way we converse with other people. Cloths and dressing influence one's confidence and also the colours combines.

Assuming a person is wearing a jeans and a t-shirt after his working hours as a Manager, his formal wear would be a 3 piece suits where his behavioural pattern is to look smart, walk smart, wear shining shoes, comb his hair and ensuring he has a clean look where else after his working hours he would like to feel loose and comfortable. He would then wear a comfortable cloth where his inter-personal skills and his behavioural pattern would change as well. Is like going to a ***"Men's Club"*** and we ought to behave decently to avoid attracting attention and causing a nuisance where else in a bar or a pub it is an open place where people are welcome with jokes, laughter and love attracting attention to themselves.

Clothing has an empowerment where is can change our character instantly and we intent to look good and comfortable with it, same goes to when a person wearing a branded clothing line such as **"VERSACE"**, the person wearing it will have a different character which will blend with the choice of clothing they wear. People who tend to wear branded clothing always have a different personality where they intent to ***"show-off"***, ***"high ego"*** and loves spending money by the way they look.

The behavioural aspect of a clothing has a personality by itself such as their texture, their colour and their branding which make a person different by wearing it. There is no harm wearing branded wear but the evolution of change in our behavioural pattern will take a different turn while wearing something good or something comfortable.

A case scenario, does an off-duty police officer with his casual wear feels confident or does he feels confident after wearing his police uniform and carry his fire arm, again the phycology of the brains tells that he feels ***"powerful"***, he feels ***"confident"*** and he feels ***"fearless"***, clothing has an impeccable value which keep us in tact with the way we dress up.

Power of the state of mind:

Understanding a state of mind is the main key to understanding change and to achieve an excellence, our behavioural is the main reason for our state of mind. How our behavioural react is how our state of mind follows. The resource on what we have is what we can do in life and sometime we will find ourselves in a resourceful state. The key to power is taking an action, every action has a chain reaction or what we try to achieve and never giving up will have a result and from that result we can work our way,to the top and achieve success.

A state can be defined as a sum of millions of neurological processes which is currently happening to us. (Anthony Robbin- Unlimited power)

The first key in redirecting your state of mind is by producing the actual result that you truly desire and how to effectively run our brain the way we want it. We have to identify what actually create a state of mind, a positive impulse which activate our brain cells to do more than others and to be more in mind control of yourself. If all the behavioural that we have is that cause of the state we are in, we might have produces different communication and behavioural pattern when we are currently at the resourceful state of mind rather be resourceful. (Anthony Robbin- Unlimited power)

There are two main components to the state of mind which is the internal representations and the second one is the condition and the use of our phycology. Simply by defining that what we say to our self and how we see the scenario picture actually puts us in a behavioural pattern of a state which we created leaving us vulnerable by other. We have to carefully control the state of mind by strengthening our emotion and telling our self-important, useful and strengthen information so our state of mind will be focus and an added advantage for us to use the resourceful we need. The main condition of our physiology actually changes the way we represent our self and how we experience the world. When we see thing difficult and tell our self that is difficult, our body will follow and will become tensed. The state we are in does determine the type of behavioural pattern we have. To control and to direct our behaviour we must always control and direct our state where we intend to go and how to reach to that particular potential is all from our state of mind. Human receive and represent information about their environment through their specialized sense of organs, there are five different sense of organ human have which are taste, smell, sight, hearing and feeling. We make most of our decision that really affect our behaviour by the use of three main senses which is visual, sights and feelings. These special receptors do transmit external stimuli to the human brain which enhance all of our senses and how we feel them. There is a very important concept when using NLP, a map is not a territory, the important note we should take note is that the characteristic of a map has to be noted and then evaluated. Successful people are able to gain access to their most resourceful state on a consistent basis. The main key of producing a result is to represent thing to yourself and to prepare your state of mind in a way that puts you in a resourceful state which empowers us that take the types and qualities of action that's creates the desire of the outcome. When we take control of our communication skills with ourselves and to produce auditory, visual and kinaesthetic signal of what we want to do, an outstanding result will be produced consistently. Human behaviour is that result of the state which we are in, we can produce the same result if our mental and physical action repeats the same action what we did before. The trigger is to give a positive vibration, a position energy and a positive say to oneself and to ensure what we thing is positive shall be made positive. (Anthony Robbin- Unlimited power)

If you were to say that you are sad and depress, the state of mind which you are in will immediately send impulse directive to the brain to change your state of mind to be sad and depressed, what we say to out body will eventually be turn to what we feel. Most humans take a very little conscious action to direct their state of mind where it fails them daily, one has to take the precautionary measure to direct your conscious mind to be firm and positive. They often wake up depressed or energized, this all happen with our state of mind, our body reacts to what we think. People who have achieve excellent are the masters of tapping into their resources part of the brain and achieving many results. Let us talk and discuss about "Datuk Tony Fernandez".

In any leadership, there is one important factor that put to test the company, earning profits is not enough in business, that it is important to create a brand or brands which will reach not only in a "Micro side" but in a "Macro Side". One believer in the power of brands is Tony Fernandes. He said it took him seven years to consciously and consistently build up the AirAsia brand name and logo as distinct and internationally known. Brands are identification marks or emblem which the life and pulse of the company. You do not need to market anything else when your branding is powerful, people will eventually look for you and market for you thru social media, word of mouth, emails, WhatsApp app and many more thru the internet.

His other traits of being a leader is in his grasp which is marketing, he is the guru of marketing where he has turn over a non-profit making airline into an active generating billion dollar industry just by using the proper marketing tools, getting the right team, listening to his staff and implementing action to get results. As a leader, your skill of marketing needs to get at its peak, hence to listen to your team of marketers on ideas which they have been absorb with different knowledge of marketing thru their

daily activities, seeing different marketing methods by different companies and doing a proper benchmark.

As in most societies, entrepreneurs cannot go against the government but need their support. Fernandes got his first ever break in year 2001 when then Malaysian Prime Minister Tun DR. Mahathir Mohamad heard of his dream and passion to start an airline and advised him. Fernandes mortgaged his house and got personal savings to buy this firm with two old jets and US$11 million worth of debt. He bought the company for one ringgit (about 26 US cents). After he turned around AirAsia, in 2003 Fernandes lobbied Dr Mahathir to raise the "Open Skies" idea with leaders of Thailand, Indonesia, and Singapore, leading to these nations giving AirAsia and other budget airlines landing rights. –"Fernandesbiodataofsuccess"

Changes in the said organization:

Fernandes has the huge believes in using digital technology for his businesses hence has generated huge amount of advantage thanks to social media. Much of his business comes from AirAsia. In fact, one unique thing about AirAsia flights is its inflight magazine **Travel 3Sixty**, which has this reminder on its page: ***"Touch me, feel me and flip me over, but you can't take me home. Read me online."*** Fernandes is not scrimping on publishing costs but this is part of his brilliant marketing strategy to make passengers discover and enjoy his website. "Fernandesbiodataofsuccess

Fernandes is famous for his personal and corporate generosity where he always gives for the unfortunate, educational funds for his staff and for others. He gives people big gifts, not only to generate loyalty to the business, but he is also generous in philanthropy.

His passion seems to be a common contribution among achievers in business, the arts, sports and other fields. Tony Fernandes loves to hire people with passion, love, honest and loyalty. He is exceptionally passionate, not only about his firms, charities and employees, but also about sports. He also owns a football team in England, an "F1" car racing team and is a major supporter of Asia's biggest mixed martial arts sport, the One FC where is enables and support those whom are interest in self-defence and health.

Tony Fernandes is a bold and crude business man but also has lots of compassion to others. He keeps himself occupied with assisting and coaching his peers to be the best of his/her abilities. He has a global and long-range vision for his various companies. As a child, he dreamt of three things in life which is having running an airline, owning an English football club and owning a Formula One racing team which has come to materialize into reality.

Fernandes has also mention that "In AirAsia we consider ourselves basically a dream factory. We deliberately decided that we wanted a company where people can pursue their passion and we wanted to make use of all the talent that we have in-house. The culture that we have already stems from the fact that we want openness and we want people to be creative and passionate about what they do. In order to do that, we've got to inspire them in every way possible and to guide them every way possible." (Fernandesbiodataofsuccess)

Positive traits that you can be learn from him:

Tony Fernandes always breaks the traditional like parent and children relationship in the organization. His workspace is an open plan workspace where nobody has rooms, hence everybody may contribute to him any idea which comes along. Everybody has a right to share an opinion and ideas with him and see thru that idea is been build up by all, the idea which he receives is always shared between his employees and peers.

He allows his employees to contact him or walk up to him on any time and he always make a statement that "do not talk behind my back, but come front and tell me directly'. All in ethics Ethnicity, age, creed and gender are not a problem in AirAsia because it is balance in harmony and racial discrimination is not welcomed. Open culture reduces the layers of bureaucracy and improve on team work and perseverance. This can reduce the time, cost and make sure the efficiency of the organization. Furthermore, it allows Fernandes to pick the right team to develop his organization, with the right team he has the full support and a benchmark where he can rely on fully. It is not about race or religion, is all about the human capability and mental state to share and contribute success over a long period of time. The human brain and committeemen once been emphasized, will greatly involve in many multi-tasking and improve on work load productivity.

Fernandes has no education or experience in managing anything about the airline industry nor the experience he had managing it. He does not care about the uncertainty risks to enter the airline industry right after the 911 terror attacks in the United States which left a suture mark and an emotional flashback.

Risk is scary but it actually gives Fernandes an opportunity to develop his talents, interests, abilities and dreams where these threats became an opportunity and strength for him to learn what he is capably are. All the method he used was (SWOT) analysis to survey his environment, the most basic fundamental business survey and management to engage in a feasibility study. He was willing to take risks to meet the challenge and finally he turned AirAsia into a profitable airline in two years with much gained experience and support.

Tony Fernandes has developed foresight that is, he succeeds to beat his competitor by providing the first budget no frills airline known as "AirAsia". He has the ability foresees the potential obstacles and tries his effort to overcome the problem as a leader. He has done brain mapping to see where his competitor will go and how to overcome an obstacle.

He plans for the future and he also can avoid the problem becoming a big issue in his organization because he always takes an action before something bad happen which is called as anticipating your next move. Is like a game of chess where you are thrill and daring to execute your move with such confidence and learning your opponent's next move.

He understands the importance of employee empowerment, he has developed the skill of employees to improve the strength of the organization as a whole. Integrity is defined as the quality of being honest, loyal and having strong moral principles. However, reliable means that the quality of being consistently good in quality or performance and also being able to be trusted by others. (Tony Fernandez-Air Asia)

The ability to learn from mistakes is not an embarrassment but it means that someone that are not afraid of facing failures, taking problems heads on will take every failure and mistake they make as a learning experience. Every entrepreneur will make mistakes and it depends is it a small or big mistake, they also fail numerous times, but each of these incidents will be a learning experience for a successful entrepreneur. Each of these instances, will be an opportunity for them to emerge better and stronger, a stepping stone for them and allows them to watch their step and step back to see what is happening.

Perceptiveness mean someone who are great at what they understanding things or figuring things out. Perceptive people are very insightful, intelligent, and able to see further what others cannot whereas perceptiveness is the ability to appreciate something of good quality. (Fernandesbiodataofsuccess)

Time is defined as indefinite continued progress of existence and events in the past, present, and future regardless as a whole while competence indicates sufficiency of knowledge and skills that allows and enable someone to act in a wide variety of situation. Because each level of responsibility has its own indecisiveness requirements, so competence can occur in any period of a person's life or at any stage of his or her career. In time, competence is a trait that shows the ability to seize all opportunities and fortune timing efficiently which will greatly improve on an individual character.

A person who is versatility defines as he or she has many different skills or qualities. Versatility permit and allows you to adapt to various situations. Versatility is also one of the important traits for a successful entrepreneur. (3airasiasuccesstrade)

Initiative is defined as someone who is taking action even though you have not been given any instructions or orders. It means meeting new and unexpected situations with prompt and fast actions which includes using resourcefulness to get something done without the normal material or methods being available to you. A real and true entrepreneur takes actions that goes beyond job boundaries or requirements or the demand of the situation. He or she creates ideas that bring about the phenomenal changes which can literarily bring success into one's mind. Generally speaking, the motivation for an initiative arises from a desire to accomplish something that would benefit the business, such as improving productivity, reducing costs, or increasing market share. Staying mentally and physically alert can improve initiative, high initiative brought higher results. Instead, if the desire to do business is not there, then obviously one cannot make a success of the venture. Certainly, an entrepreneur must show the initiative to attain results. (3airasiasuccesstrade)

The traits that bring Tony as a successful entrepreneurship because he has a foresight thinking man. According to Tony, his secret of success comes from his thoughts, mind body and soul that always mention "Dream the Impossible". (Tony Fernandez-Air Asia) Example that shows that Tony Fernandes is a foresight person is when he makes a decision to buy the loss-making Air Asia and then transformed it from a small and struggling airline and become one of the fastest growing and most successful low fare airlines in the world. Despite of all the negativity surrounding Tony, he was also able to look past all of that as he saw even greater opportunity after the tragedy of 911 that aircraft rental costs dropped by 40% as a result of tragedy of 911. (Tony Fernandez- Air Asia) Experienced staff were also much more readily because aviation companies were laying-off their staff and fear of the failing economy. (Successfulltraitstonyfernandes)

Tony Fernandes concern about his employee and realize that human resource is important in driving an organization profit and revenue. He embraces the work ethics of "walk-around" management style, trusts in working with the employees and work with his staff every few days each month.

Decentralizing authority and anti-hierarchy will result in quick communication and increase the productivity of the workforce. He has successfully built a good relationship with his colleagues where it can create loyalty toward the company and low turnover rates where what training he has given will not be lost. Employees will forever stay in AirAsia due to its remarkable employer's affection. This will create a talented cooperation between colleagues and to move toward organization goal and to success.

Fernandes has received awards for the "Visionaries & Leadership Series". He communicates a vision very vigorously: ***"Dream the impossible, believe the unbelievable, and never take no for an answer". (Tony Fernandez- Air Asia)***

He takes the high risks and optimistic in achieving his dream. He introduces "Low Cost Airline", He also created the "first" in Asia by starting a hotel chain, Tune Hotels which is based on the no-frills concept, cheap and easy. All of this amazing entrepreneurship all have been achieve by believe the impossible, take advantage of the possibility and make it your own. (Anthony Robbins-Unlimited Power)

He was aided by Dr Mahathir to raise the idea with the leaders of neighbouring Thailand, Indonesia, and Singapore and eventually to be successful in getting the landing rights to AirAsia and other discount carriers. All of this was his initiative to be successful but all he needed was a very good mentor, networking skills and good command in communication. His knowledge of human behaviour is superior and he understand how to use it to his full resources and gaining a potential benchmark.

To be a visionary allows him become to be sensitive toward what is happening in the business environment, so they will take the quick action to deal with the opportunity or treat exist. This will enable him to take risk, become enterprise and expanding his horizon.

Many of the competitor with Tony at the time said this wasn't aviation's moment and that he would fail miserably. Every other airline in the world was scaling back and cutting overhead due to their respectful budgets, while AirAsia was cutting fares. Fernandes struggled to secure investor confidence and their financial backing and none of the international banks were prepared to help him except one, Credit Suisse's involvement with AirAsia began in the year 2002 where they confidently and privately funded a $30 million placement that laid the groundwork to propel AirAsia upward. Quickly, AirAsia not only became profitable, but also expanded, with more airplanes, new routes, and a second hub at Senai Johor International Airport.

In a little over a year, Credit Suisse has helped AirAsia grow into Asia's largest low-cost carrier, flying approximately 45 million passengers a year to more than 80 destinations. AirAsia has grown from a Malaysian domestic airline to the largest low-cost carrier in Asia in terms of their fleet size and passengers carried, what began with an initial investment of less than a dollar is now an airline group with a market cap of $2.1 billion. An entrepreneur must be the person that must have the ability to arrange their time management wisely so that they can compete with the other entrepreneur in grabbing the opportunity occurred for their business. To be a great leader, time factor is one of the most important things in the entrepreneurial world of business. If the entrepreneur cannot arrange their time, they might lose and mitigate their chances in the opportunity for their business and these will make they lose in their business. Tony Fernandez has become a mentor for all business enthusiasm and confidently making his name in the history book for the world to see.

Learning and research about Tony Fernandez has become an inspiration for everyone, how he showered himself with unlimited resources of knowledge is the way he creates his state of mind, his mind set has been set. His resources which he has unlimited gained is always available to him because of the mind-set which he sets for himself.

CHAPTER 5

Does Emotion improve Customer care and profitability

The word emotion has a thousand meaning which relates to the human behaviour, it is a surge of impulse and character which fuels the human body with feeling, touch, listening, tasting and looking. Selling a product in any establishments is not pretty simple, it need several training and the focus on how to upsell certain product such as "Hotel rooms" or "Promotional Food and Beverage Menu" which is very difficult to sell, getting the rich and famous to buy this item is not very easy even they are loaded with cash. Is the mechanism of how to illustrate the product and services rendered offer by the specific establishment?

As author of "Unlimited Power"- Anthony Robbin may describe it as an emotion is a burst of expression by the human brain, it needs the body senses to send an impulse to the brain where is then filtered and express feeling such as smile, interest, taste, sights and listening. All this impulses has a chemical neuron which feed information to the brain which then tells the body on how to react on this impulse, example of an impulse when we take a bite of a sweet delicious chocolate cake, the chemical impulses send to our main cortex on how to manage this feeling. It then filters and send control impulses back to our sense of taste, feeling, sight and smell. How do human respond to a delicious piece of cake, they will eventually change their state of mind imagining how the taste of the cake will be like and the smell of the cake.

Emotion are very important to the human body where it reacts to all of our Neuro senses and transport to an impulse of sensation feelings, this feeling is then incorporated with our sense of judgement.

It has shown that when a waiters tries out several food testing, they will experience a burst of flavours in their mouth where chemical neuron sending impulses to the brain telling them how to react to this feeling, the body will always acts on its emotion by the smell of the food, the taste and the presentation of the food. This emotion acts as a benchmark of themselves where it helps define and explain to customers how they enjoyed the food and the pleasure of having it. This comes under "Neuro Linguistic Programming"-Anthony Robbins, where you are currently programming an individual the state of mind and the experience of your gastro food odyssey journey.

A practise has been done with several staff and customer in the hotel where an emotional measurement of ratio has been conducted, a basic study of research on how an emotional can be measured using the same fundamental studies of (SWOT) but adding an additional factor to it. This can be used for personal benchmark as well as in the hospitality industry.

The research was amazing and many of the test subject were curious on how their emotional ration can be measured using this technique. They were given a question which affect their emotion with a scale from 1 which is weak and 5 is the strongest.

"Sharma Emotional Measurement Ration"

S	W
T	O

Question 1:

On the word "Strength" what is the emotional feeling you have affecting you, please give five answers where "1" is the weakness and "5" is the strongest.

No	"Strength" Emotional Feeling	Measurement of feelings
1	Family Bonding	5
2	Careers	5
3	Education	5
4	Dependable	5
5	Family safety	5
	Total	**25**

Question 2:

On the word "Weakness" what is the emotional feeling you have affecting you, please give five answers where "1" is the weakness and "5" is the strongest.

No	"Weakness" Emotional Feeling	Measurement of feelings
1	Losing a family member	5
2	Careers	4
3	Friendship	2
4	Relationship	3
5	Knowledge	3
	Total	**17**

Question 3:

On the word "Opportunity" what is the emotional feeling you have affecting you, please give five answers where "1" is the weakness and "5" is the strongest.

No	**"Opportunity" Emotional Feeling**	**Measurement of feelings**
1	Business Opportunity	5
2	Career	5
3	Financial	5
4	Exploration	5
5	Family Bonding	5
	Total	**25**

Question 4:

On the word "Threat" what is the emotional feeling you have affecting you, please give five answers where "1" is the weakness and "5" is the strongest.

No	**"Threat" Emotional Feeling**	**Measurement of feelings**
1	Business Competition	3
2	Careers	4
3	Financial	4
4	Family Safety	5
5	Failures	5
	Total	**21**

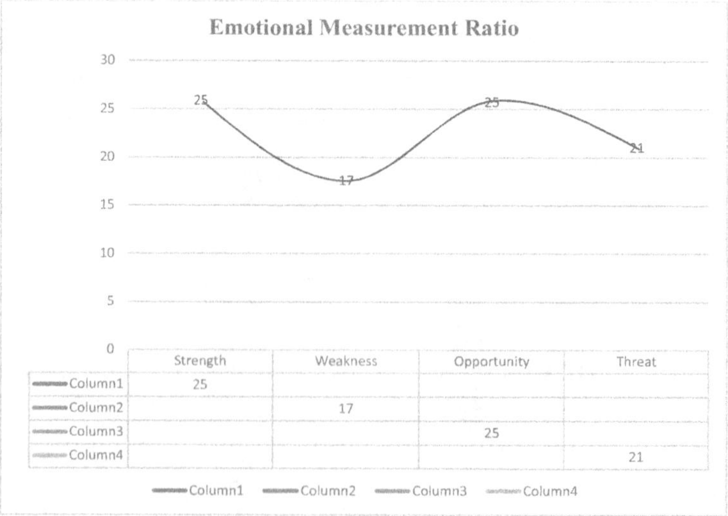

In the **"Emotional Measurement Ratio"** explain that this person has a balance "Strength" and "Opportunity" which make this person a strong will individual and is determine to set his mind set and determine his journey to success. His emotional weakness is being control with logic which dictates that he is in control of his behaviour and this individual shows a minimal expression of emotion. The emotional feeling such as weakness is normal for every human being on the matter on how they control their feeling and suggestions. The conclusion also explain that he also has a "weakness" but is closely measured to what the weakness is related to, the weakness can be measured with personal affection, at the work place or his family time. Hence to the "Threat" related aspect, this individual knows his competition and has prepared to overcome the obstacle.

This measurement ratio has been used and experimented with employees and customers of a "Resort" known as "Coco hut Long Beach Resort, Pulau Perhentian Terengganu. Different people have a different experience using this ***"EMR"- Emotional Measurement Ratio"*** which specify on their emotional measurement.

Hence this will be appropriate to be used in any staff appraisal where we can use the main core as ***"Emotional", "Progressive", "Teamwork" or "Attitude"*** where it has the ability to measure one's performance index.

With the use of this **"EMR"** it is likewise to say that, this method will improve customer's satisfaction and profitability and has an added advantage, this ensures that employees are measured correctly with their sense of responsibility, attitude and committeemen.

According to a research done by Michele McGovern that if we as human do not use emotional as a main key to build customer loyalty that we are just wasting our time. Customers whom are very emotionally attached to a product or services intend to purchase and spend more on their desired product rather than satisfies customers. An emotional customer always purchases the same product or same brand where they are confident are emotionally attached to the brand due to branding and styles. What is define as emotional connection, it has to do a lot by capturing the heart and mind of the customers, getting their loyalty will not be easy but once they are emotionally attached due to the services given, they will always come back.

(Michele McGovern – Customer Experience Insights)

An example, why do customers frequently come back to a hotel bar or to dine in a restaurant where they can always have their food and beverage elsewhere is cheaper and affordable. Those customers are emotionally attached to the place due to its services, they are always comfortable with the atmosphere, the music which is played and how the services staff treat them which makes them feel they are the king. Customers feels a sense of loyalty once they get to know the owner and their staff where services are given uniquely where everyone is been treated equally but with full heartedly. Giving an emotional driven service always make a customer come back for more, customers feels is better to speak to a service staff where they are never judge but only to lend a ear so their customers may feel comfortable. Customers continue to but because service staff fills their desire and passion to buy and to feel secure.

(Michele McGovern – Customer Experience Insights)

Brands usually puts million into boosting awareness, satisfaction, loyalty but they always overlook the most important of all the main recipe which is "emotional connection". Customers always connect emotionally with brands which make them stand out of the crowd, makes them feel secure, make them feel important, improve their personal feeling and to make them look confident. (Scott Magids, Alan Zorfas, Daniel Leemon- Harvard Business Reviews)

The main benefits in measuring emotion in customer experience is to identify the importance of their interest and to gain perspective into what product and services needed which can generate profitability. Emotional intelligent or also known as emotional quotient has been linked with the performance of the company employees and the success which includes customer's retention, increase in sales, increase productivity in leadership management and marketing. (Keisha Stoute-Emotional Intelligence)

The word emotional intelligence is defined as being aware of our own emotion and how to control that feeling of emotion and to be mindful with our surroundings, hence this gives a very clear indication that emotional intelligence allows us to isolate a positive feeling and how to disburse that feeling properly. In fact, this method of using emotional intelligence will give the employees the confidence hence getting a progressive rate of return by selling the product and services. There are four most important emotional awareness skills which is mostly been used to develop and to increase sales and profitability which is ***"Personal Awareness", "Personal Management", "Social Awareness"*** and ***"Relationship Management".***

Personal Awareness:

Is defined to being awareness of our emotions and how is likely to manifest with the reaction or a trigger towards our self. This manifestation can be positive and negative which an impact has been created by a certain problem, an interesting excitement or a actual case scenario which would reflect the brain to react. In the hospitality industry, controlling our personal awareness can be challenging due to the differentiation of ethnicity, culture and internal issues where is may be justified by an irritated and rude customer. (Keisha Stoute-Emotional Intelligence)

Personal awareness also associates with feelings such as flavours of food or a cold tasty beverage which indulge with our feeling of being satisfied, hence this proclaimed the emotional feeling of such of having an added advantage in our life where is hugely beneficial in work ethics.

Personal Management:

This is defined as how we manage our emotional and how to effectively place or use the positive emotion using the right method. (Keisha Stoute-Emotional Intelligence)

Applying positive emotion enables us to perform our jobs better hence giving us the quality and branding deserved. This applies on our customers service skills as well where using the positive emotion assist us in achieving the possible creating opportunities for the future.

Social Awareness:

Once you have personally achieve on how to control our emotion, it is easier to identify others who are incapable of managing their emotion hence giving you the opportunity to take advantage of the situation whereby controlling the scenario on the tip of your palm where you are able to calm matters down and solve various problem and to achieve a satisfaction that you are capable of managing various emotion and utilizing them.

Relationship Management:

Relationship management is an area of expertise where you are able to take the opportunity of your awareness and take control of emotion of others to develop and maintain relationship. Hence this enables you to take full control of the conversation and able to close various deals. Taking full control of other conversation and emotion and making it your skills which needs to be trained and developed, this skill will be able to be used in any industry where closure of any deal will be a positive inspiration. Relationship Management allows us to secure our potential clients and able to manipulate the outcome by using their emotion and ensuring it is done in the correct way, hence this will also be associated with Neuro linguistic programming where the art of suggestions is always available to others.

Do Emotion effects Tonality?

In the search for profitability growth organization, more and more companies are investing in connecting with customer care and their feedback experience, they are willing to spend more to understand the growth in business by customers experience and their emotional response. The investment is the result of studies and research done by companies such as branding, product and services, customers experience, product quality, product which has an emotional effect on their customers and promotion which will eventually increase profitability and sales. (Harvard Business Review – Mei 2016)

Most companies are lacking of strategic objectives which can heighten the customer's journey and experience which will bring an end result of increase of customer's satisfaction and increase of customer's value. Many companies are getting sources and information by the use of secondary data collection on their customer's feasibility studies and demographic studies and trying to monopolize their existing customers. Their main goal is to improve on customer's satisfaction with their journey and experience. The most effective way to improve and maximize customer experience is to go beyond customer's satisfaction and go into customer's emotional level where by tapping into their fundamental motivation and fulfilling their deep emotional level which are unspoken emotional needs. (Harvard Business Review – Mei 2016)

The customers experience is an important driver in getting customers emotion and their desire to fulfil their needs and wants.

How emotional connection is helping companies by increasing their sales profit, there are four major important steps where we can get the most of this by tapping into the customer's emotion.

Determine the emotion creating the customers value in a business?

Tapping into customer's emotion and trigger a physiological effect in determining for them to buy your products, services and to be a loyal customer's. Through the use of anticipation or predictive decision, this will increase the sales profit, customers growth and sales will be quantifying. (Scott Magids – Chief Executive May 2016)

Applying an emotion to the customer's experience?

The more the company taps into a customer's emotion, the higher chance for them to gain profits, customer's value, and customer experience and customers growth.

(Scott Magids – Chief Executive May 2016)

For an example, if we look at "Mydin Malaysia" their marketing is to ensure the family gets the best products, cheap, affordable and always giving what customers want. They take an extra mile to do monthly surveys and to gain loyalty and confident by their customer's. "Mydin Melaka" has open more than 100 chains in Malaysia and they are the biggest chain ever in Malaysia, by understanding customers value, by emphasising on their believe and by giving back to their customers with the use of Cash Vouchers during festive seasons with the use of their customer's data base. "Mydin Melaka" has become a "Trusted Brand" in Malaysia where all their loyal customers know that their pricing is always lower and affordable and always being meticulously with their customer's emotion.

Targeting the customers who will show most of their efforts?

In each of any industry, customers are more emotional towards certain product which a company's carries, targeting them would be

an added advantage and engaging with these customers may yield significant "ROI" on acquisition investment.
(Scott Magids – Chief Executive May 2016)

"Primary Data Collection" is always important to know where our market segments are and how to achieve it, a detail "SWOT Analysis" is always advisable and can assist to achieve various obstacle. Recruiting a "Risk Analysis" which involves researching market segments and ratio analysis is always important, a proper consultant needs to be brought in, certain time is best to use a neural approach where internal factors may conflict the data collecting due to emotional constraints and internal problems such as politics.

Targeting and identifying a potential client is always not easy where putting a right employee to collect the data is important, getting a professional with people skills and great customer care is always important in getting a good data collection. Using the method of "RM 1.00" to get a potential client will be the best way in solving a problem which has been used and experimented in various hotel.

The method is been used as for every "RM 1.00" how do we bring in a potential customer and what equipment will we utilized. Using the "RM 1.00" theory is by utilizing the "RM 1.00" into a budget for one person by breaking down. Below is the example of budget which will be utilized for a potential customer.

Exhibit 1: Budget Sample Utilization for "RM 1.00" (Roy Prasad)

No	Description	(RM) Amount	Remarks
1.	Brochure	RM 0.15	Printed in thousands.
2.	Telephone call made	RM 0.20	Telemarketing done by staffs
3.	Administration efforts	RM 0.20	Office works and management
4.	Marketing Department	RM 0.20	Designing and graphics
5.	Man Power	RM 0. 25	Efforts put into
	Total	**RM 1.00**	

To measure the value of the emotions:

All leading brands measure their customer's similarly like a (KPI) "Key Performance index". The critical measurement of your brand can be measured through several key surveys to identify emotional behaviour towards a certain product and what are the attachment does other customers have. All brands have an history impact which primary data and secondary data collection is advisable to be consider to collect relevant information and to create a new data entry database to measure the index of interest for each product.

(Scott Magids – Chief Executive May 2016)

In the United Kingdom, "Mark & Spencer's" always perform a primary data collection and secondary data collection where they serve the customers what they like, called it like a creative personal shopping mall where every customers have their favourite things, that's why they are capable of changing fresh produce every day. This company has been serving their public on what is important to them and giving them cost cutting expenses, branded brand world-wide and every single individual has a favourite item which is known as "Personalize Favourite Chart" where surveys has been done for almost 20 years where they give the best of service to all and there is no favouritism in their business, everybody is treated equally.

Most of all major decision we make in a split second are based on our human emotion, they are a base layer of neural circuitry underpinning rational deliberation. As for our race and culture, we meet and judge people within a period of "7 seconds" where we do not give time to evaluate possibilities and perception which are hidden. We as human choose the cloths we wear and what car we drive based on other people perception on us, how they look at us is how we try to be what they aspect of. (Ticket Stripe- Marketing and Promotion)

By relying more on our snap decision power by using emotions, we conserve our brain computing power by more important factors such as "when to pick-up the kids" or "what is for dinner". (Ticket Stripe- Marketing and Promotion)

When we look at the world's greatest company like "Four Seasons", "Hilton" and "Shang-Ri La" we think they are the coolest of all, what set the different with other companies and how can they achieve a great culture with a great game plan. This can be measured on how motivated they are and the team which creates these motivational games and the types of benefits when performance level meets their "KPI", and it is not always about high salary. The surrounding culture of the organization set a whole new atmosphere where working has become an exciting game play where everyone wants a piece of the challenge no matter which type of department you are in. Motivation is not just a touchy feeling when you need it to be, in fact according to studies done by ***"Harvard Business Review"*** motivation can great benefit a company and organization by 47%. (Breena Kerr- 2015)

"HBR" or known as "Harvard Business Review" has looked at three motivator mechanics which comprises the reason to work with, the one which makes people more motivated, proactive, resilient, and productive. The breakdown is below:

The Good:

Play, Purpose and Potential

Play:

Play actually happens when an individual is excited, passionate and enjoys the job they do which makes them evenly excited and confident. They do not feel and look at it as work, they feel it is a game for them where they enjoy their work so much and by improving their performance and "KPI" every day following the "Kaizen" term. An individual look at their work as a game where they dance to their tempo while enjoying every minute of it where urges the company to make them an asset, a driving individual which drive and strive through the company with passion and perseverance. (Breena Kerr- 2015)

Purpose:

The word purpose defines as when in critical time your work means something, where it is important at the crucial time. It is an identity which meet a purpose to be needed and to ensure the task and job is been completed. Example of a purpose would define as "The purpose of your position as a manager is to ensure the happiness of our customer's and to ensure you are comfortable with your job scope which makes you very happy. The purpose of that position also depicts or define your individuality as an asset for the company, meaning that the company has selected you for a bigger purpose, to create your own personal brand and to ensure your purpose for the company meets your goal in life. (Breena Kerr- 2015)

Potential:

Potential is defined where you work you put and add on your own personal attributes, your additional abilities to ensure to work is done correctly and responsibilities are in concern. Doing more on a works will ensure there is an opportunity for a next phase in your career for enhancement and a higher salary. Potential is always given an award by major companies because this potential is natural and can be groomed by major players.
(Breena Kerr- 2015)

The Bad:

Emotionally Pressured:

This is defined as when you are working for something external which threated you as you are trying to prove yourself or afraid that you are not doing a proper job. This makes you leave focus on the actual task where you are too busy thinking how to impress others, yourself or by taking into a competition for a higher position and salary. The problem with this type of motivation keep the individual in peer pressure, in fear and does not focus properly on his capabilities and they are often disconnected for their focus. (Breena Kerr- 2015)

Economically Pressured:

In this area, is define when a compensation makes you work for something short term, this motivation clearly removes you from your focus for a long-term career. The career path you have chosen Working with this motivation makes you lose your identity where people makes an identity for yourself whereby working for a compensation such as Over-time or extra leave is added in. (Breena Kerr- 2015)

Inertia:

This is the worst motivation ever where you are on an auto pilot mode, what work you have done yesterday you are repeating in over and over again. Loosing focus, identity and passion hence keeping you careers from progressing. (Breena Kerr- 2015)

This has the capabilities to lose your identity. This way of motivation is the merest poor in training an individual where creating his career would be merely impossible, their job is just one which is making a cup of coffee for their bosses every day. This kind of motivation should not be used at all in any industry where is does not create any opportunity or careers, this hereby creates a dead zone where there is no use in any business or hospitality sector.

Tonality of voice effecting our mood with our emotion:

When he speaks and listen to people communicating, we can surely hear whether they are sad, angry, emotional, happy, cranky, depressed, bored and nervous just by the sound of their voice. Studies has also been shown by ***"lead-author Jean –Julien Aucouturier, Ph.D.- French National Centre for Scientific Research" (CNRS)- France*** that we are doing this to ourselves by the way we speak that follows our emotional mood. (Traci Pedersen)

An experiment has been done where selected individual is requested to read out loud while hearing and by listening to their own voice which are altered to sound happy, sad and fearful by the use of a headset.***Julien Aucouturier, Ph.D. - French National Centre for Scientific Research" (CNRS) - France***

The individual or volunteer test subjects were shocked with their finding that they were unaware that their voice is being manipulated. This is to suggest that people do not know always and understand how to control their voice and their emotion for every specific goal, their voices are being manipulated. (Traci Pedersen)

The frequency of our tone of voice is different others and the way we listen it to ourselves, this frequency does manipulate through our feeling of emotions which triggers an chain reaction where all emotions are bursting out hence having control our behaviour and the way we speak clearly can be identifies by others.

CHAPTER 6

When there is no "Effective Communication" what are the criteria of problems

Anytime one party misunderstand or wrongly understands a communication can cause many frictions and potentially to create problems. Poor communication is very frustrating which can lead to poor performance, lack of team work and have a low morale which can reduce profits.

(Lisa McQuerrey) The art of communication is so powerful that wrongly presented or communicated wrongly can lead to many severe problems, it can lead a good team from break up which cause the effectiveness to gain profit will be disrupted. A good team what keeps an establishment in Par Level with other establishment, how the team market products and advertise a product will eventually get their loyal customers seeking for a new product. Emotional attachment to purchase new product, clients are very comfortable with their personal favourite seller, they always complement them, give them extra freebie and always makes the sale because of the customer loyalty program where the customers always trust the salesman.

Communications is a fact of life where it is essential for all human being from small ages to adults. When the communication is not being delivered, many problems such as failures, profits, employees depressed and lack of personality traits, this failure can affect the personal traits and business of an establishment. Several problems will occur which will seriously affect the company, losses will begin then comes the high employee turnover, and employees will have no passion to work anymore due to the effectiveness of communication which causes many problems.

When the command of communication is not being trained properly, negative issues and assumptions are created within the organization which causes friction with all employees. There are nine cause of communication breakdown which occurs in any establishments which are ***"Unmet Expectations", "Stress in Workplace", "Relational Breakdown", "Low Morale", "Dissatisfied Clients", "The Bottom Line", "Family Issues", "Health" and "Improving Communication".***

Unmet Expectation:

Without a clear communication, it is not clear or to prioritised which task to do first and where to start, it is also difficult to communicate with the group.

Normally a Project Manager is selected but without constant communication it will be difficult to finish the project and getting to know last minute changes by the clients.

The lack of communication causes an unmet expectation where lots of confusion occurs within the group. Lots of assumption which are not related begins to arise, such errors like team miss deadlines and client miss their appointment and people on project does not know what their roles are. (Anne Kinsey March 2018)

Stress in Workplace:

High stress level ion the work place are huge problem of communications problems, a poor communication seems like everything you are doing is very urgent and causing yourself and other to hurry which cause mistakes to occur. An unhealthy communication causes fear that causes tension. (Anne Kinsey March 2018)

Relational Breakdown:

This occurs where we receive email or orders with a different tone of voice, accusation or finger pointing which normally caused in an establishment. This normally occurs when a person does not want to share or sit down to find solution on a problem and hiding behind the desk.
(Anne Kinsey March 2018)

Low Morale:

When a person spends more time on emotional, they usually spend time on emotional management, productivity goes down and their morale goes lower than usual.
(Anne Kinsey March 2018)

When business relationship is wounded, trust goes out the window and eye to eye contact will be difficult to comprehend. Positivity in the workplace would be affected hence productivity would be affected producing bad result in profits and performance.

Dissatisfied Clients:

Dissatisfied client can be the reason of a very poor communication, not meeting a dateline or missing an appointment. These occurrences normally occur when a contract has been closed but the service is not given to a proper attention hence the reason of being is due to poor communication within the department and to your team. (Anne Kinsey March 2018)

A customer's deadline is very important, working together and having a proper communication and constantly updating the progress is a good start to achieve a good relationship.

A customer's satisfaction begins from confronting a client with a project, planning the project with them, introducing your team, working on a concept and a budget and mitigating extra cost expenses is what makes the client to be trust worthy of you.

The Bottom Line:

When customers are dissatisfied with your products and services, customers always look elsewhere where they can get a better service which can cause your company to lose money. Even looking at a legality point of view that customers sues the company because of discriminating towards them such as services provide and the product which does not seem correct which cause the company to lose money. A poor communication can lead to a very high turnover for employees which cause a high cost to hiring and training where the company keeps on losing money. (Anne Kinsey March 2018)

Family Stress:

Employee who goes home often are worn out and unable to spend time with their family which causes a conflict. Often, they feel they have been neglected which causes their spouses to question

them on time to spend with them which leads to arguments. Often employees will fell the conflict hence causes them into depression which causes their work performance to be question where their performance would be disrupted due to a heavy stress and conflict they have at home. It is always good to have a pleasant work where good communication skills and the way the employer looks after their employees.
(Anne Kinsey March 2018)

Having a stress-free environment and following the constitution of the legal system of labour law would help prevent this from reoccurring. Family often wonder why their spouse have no time for their family which causing a big question, “Look for another Job” hence looking for a new job will not be easy, challenges occur when working for a long time in a company then starting back from scratch will cause another personality depression unless you have a very good recommendation by your peers.

Health:

Often personal matter arises when your health is in concern when going back home and coming to work, high stress level can cause many fatal diseases which may harm the human body. Most occurrences are always “Strokes”, “Heart Complication”, “Sleep deprivation” and “High Fevers”. Employee does not have the proper “Emotional Management Skills” to manage their day to day life styles. Working to long could cause exhaustion where proper management of working time has to be establishment to ensure all staff gets enough rest.
(Anne Kinsey March 2018)

Family and their spouses would be in concern for their health as they are the provider for financial and food on the table, hence family will also be in an emotional state concerning on their spouses whom are having health issues which may jeopardise their family relations.

Improving Communication:

If communication is poor, in which it can impact on stress level, health issues, the bottom line, dissatisfied client and family issues, it is better to improve on communication such as writing them the top priorities, sending email and text message and also helps to often visit them to see their progress. Let them know you are there to assist and help them to avoid these problems. Manage their time efficiently where they rest time is balance and priorities their job where they are able to complete their task which are top priorities. Certain employee communication is bad that it is difficult for them to communicate and to relay their messages. Those employees who has personal issues in the work place sometimes feel embarrassed to communicate between their peers and to their management on the issue which they have. Those issues are the main reason why their solution has not been concluded hence delaying the possibility of a severe stress culture at the work place. High turn-over normally persist and also health complication often occurs in the work place. The management should take their responsibilities to identify flaws and employee problem and to investigate what is the occurrences for their sudden behaviour.

Always send good and calm messages to them and allow them to see you as a friend and not as a strict boss. The respect should be there where they can identify you as a boss but understand that you are also a friend which depends on them to finish their task. Have a game with them which included active listening skills and coach them on how to properly communicate efficiently. Explaining to them when communication us properly done, there will have no problems in personal issues or grudges. Solve the internal matters like grudge and jealously by calming the situation down by calling all the employees and solving the problems instead of keeping quiet and not talking. Treat your employees with kindness and give them top priorities on what you need them to do and ensure they have their skills job on hand and what they are good at. Once they are comfortable with each other and how they communicate then the advance level for "cross-training" would be sufficient for them to handle since they know their jobs and they know the colleagues. (Anne Kinsey March 2018)

It is always good to sit down with them daily and have a chat, find problems and solve it, treat employee with kindness and making sure that they careers are being observe of the company to grow them together will make a lot of thing clearer.

Communication issues often occur when they are from different region where their dialect and tonality is different. Ensuring their tone is spoken clearer and slower will help break the ice and allow others to listen and understand. Handling human behaviour needs experience and sometimes you need to coordinate with a physiologist to ask him or her advice on how to manage your employees.

It is good to always have an outing with them to see how they express themselves, visit their homes to see how they live and play with their children which gives an full emotional attachment, trust and loyalty towards you because the employers take the time to visit them at home.

Some problem of ineffective listening skills is those whom are having problem in effective listening skills, use of inappropriate medium, poor message conceptualization and general lack of trust. The first cause arises when the sender uses the wrong communication styles and express their thoughts wrongly and inadequately, hence this makes the receiver does not understand the message correctly and able to interpret it properly. The receiver is in confusion when he is unable to anticipate the message or decipher the message. Failing to give relevant information such as email, text, letter of instruction can give lots of confusion when the information is not correctly explained, also grammatical errors do cause confusion to the reader failing to anticipate the instruction or message. Choosing the wrong medium such as social media message system, email or fax can also complicate thing even more when proper instruction is not given, reader may conclude the wrong message and act upon it, this is where it is necessary for the sender to explain properly in details and also

to choose the right person to receive the message and distribute the message accordingly.
(Maurice Odine-School of Journalism & Graphic Communication)

The second matter is that the company or organization experience a severe distrust and low morale of the employees which will cause a high friction with the clash of culture when different background fails to acknowledge and value differences in the workplace. The third is that managers fails to assess their communication skills, not having proper training in communication may distribute miscommunication with the staff, one simple misinterpreted message can be misunderstood and hence began a rumour in the establishment assessing the company does not k now how to talk due to the tonality and the messages been send wrongly. If a message is sent to a highly emotional employee, the message will be interpreted wrongly hence causing an emotional feeling amongst the employees.
(Maurice Odine-School of Journalism & Graphic Communication)

Problem of ineffective communication:

There are several problems to an ineffective communication where is derived from the hospitality industry and other business establishments, these may be risen to the complexity of ways of communication amongst peers and employees.
(Neil Kokemuller- September 2017)

This ineffectiveness usually brings issues such as ***"mistrust", "loyalty", "committeemen", "anxiety", "careers", "voluntary", "vision", "mission", "being one", connect with your staff", and "Being an example".***

Mistrust:

An effective employee usually causes jealousy in the establishment where the most favourite of creating a rumour is "character assassination" where is to make the favourite into a worst employee by crashing an individual spirit and motivation. Company often have this gossip where the company has to appoint a "relationship manager" to clear all problem amongst employee and get to the bottom of the problem.

When a company starts to listen to the gossip and start to believe in it, it will create a effect which will destroy the committeemen of an individual which the gossip leads to and even tarnish their trust towards the company. A person whom has been accused as distrust will feel to be kept away and just keeping quiet and not speaking to anybody, the feeling is disastrous which eventually cause an emotional shut down. The suspicious will be turn into an obsession where something which is really not there is been trying to prove it is there, hence proclaiming that the person is wrong, a rumour or gossip turn into an accusation and the determination to destroy an individual future for the sake of a gossip. The individual whom has been accused as a distrust will eventually feel that the company has betrayed him just because for an accusation towards him since he was the hardest working employee in that establishments, a jealous party may want to destroy his career just to be ahead of him.
(The effect of distrust in our relationship-November 3 2017-Emotions)

Loyalty:

Loyal employees are able to contribute extra on their job duties, performance and ideas, for them the company is like home and the employer should respect and motivate the employees even more by giving extra benefits and special attention towards them, also not to forget to give a special attention to other employee hoping they will gain loyalty to you and your company. Getting an employee to be loyal to you will not be easy, it is all about giving the respect they deserve and taking the extra mile to ask them about their career life, their family and their health whether is there any issue of health problem working here such as stress, migrant, and body ache. If a company which produces food and beverage such as hotels, the employees are making part of themselves by using the branding of the company which makes it a signature dish, customer who are galvanised with the taste and presentation of the food always stay loyal not only to the company but to the employee who actually made the food production, as before we have given example of the apple pie where customers do enjoy quality and taste. The employee are producing product and service on behalf of the company which makes them as a stakeholder as well, the management ought to keep the company branding at high peak where employee may look proud that they are working for such a company with good reputation, good branding and a family oriented management where they adore career enhancement and productivity. There are four important ways of building an employee loyalty which is crucial in the productivity of any establishments, as below will be identifies and explain thoroughly. These finding is very important to be used in engaging staff which loyalty is most of important in an organization.

Committeemen:

A proper committeeman from the employee, the company will gain more productivity, good ideas and good team work with a positive effect in the company. Working as a team will gain more success when the employer and employee shares the same vision, collective feeling and trust in a group. According to ***"Kevin Eikenberry"*** on his ***"Eye On Sales"*** article, there are three types of "Team Committeemen", a good leadership and a shared vision always entrust the performance of the employer and employee.
(eyesonsales.com/author/kevin_eikenberry)
(smallbusiness.chron.com/effects-team-commitment-42028.html)

Shared Responsibilities:

Team work meaning to take another person responsibility when another team worker is off duty or on leave, here is where the team effort to add another responsibility to their agenda where working together is the best option to resolve the situation and the additional duties.

The team realizes that team work enable the performance and working as a team benefits the company and their commitment to work as a team. Team work will also realise that the work they put it will be thoroughly and meticulously detail because of team effort to depend on each other to finish the task.
(eyesonsales.com/author/kevin_eikenberry)
(smallbusiness.chron.com/effects-team-commitment-42028.html)

Retention:

High staff turn-over is bad for business and it effects the progress of the company, effect the moral of other employees and cost in both recruitment and training from the company. A happy staff will not only stay longer, they will even improve their performance and improve their committeemen, moral and loyalty. This will eventually increase the progress of the company when retention on employees are done correctly and progressively.

There are several areas which can boost employee retention and increase the progress of the company in internal employees benefit. Listed below are the most effective way for employee retention.

Cost savings:

Currently recruitment fees are expensive where going through the company resource to allocated and select a recruitment company and going through resume takes time where is best spend in improving the company. Setting up training required lots of expenses where we are unable to anticipate will the new employee stay or leave in a short time.

By adding an additional expense is best to invest back in the company by training existing employees and increasing their benefits which will allow an increase of progress where improvement in communication and sales can be an abundance of increase when trained properly.

Experience employees:

An experience staff gains more experience when they have worked for your company more than 2 years, they are able to bring up to speed with new recruits and allow them to performed better with proper training or improved training which they have gained knowledge from when using their experience but not to go out of the "SOP" guidelines. Their ability to be a mentor for the new recruits will be an added bonus where you will not need to hire external consultant or to pay additional cost to Human Resource to organize training, experience are the best way to improve a company and the new employees, experience staff are an asset for the company where they have the knowledge of the company and understand the scope and vision of the company. When the company does not show the respect needed for the experience staff or give accreditation towards the experience employee such as promotion, increase benefits or increment of salary, they are likely to go elsewhere, the employees will be given a better salary and scope of benefit, added to that they will even bring the experience to your competitor which will tarnished your business.
(Corporaterewards.com.uk-advantages-of-employee-retention)

Loyalty:

A longstanding employee will be more loyal then a new comers and their performance will be exemplary. Longstanding staff understand the vision, mission and the purpose of the business where they are headed to for the future. They want what is best for the business since they have develop a long relation trust with the company, managers, employer and their peers which makes them an efficient teams, motivating them will be easier based on their passion and what the employers sees in them, happier employee tend to do more and perform better when they are happy in an establishment. The best of all is that a happier staff tend to perform well and better to progress the speed of the company efforts and to support their peers on their next shifts.
(Corporaterewards.com.uk-advantages-of-employee-retention)

Workplace culture:

A work culture that has a high rate of staff turn-over may give the impression towards their staff that staff are simple easier to replace when needed. The happier and more uplifted your staff is, the better the workplace culture tends to be, ultimately creating a friendly atmosphere for other staff to perform better, motivated staff are able to motivate their peers due to how they feel towards the company. Often advisable to have staff function once a month to ensure they are relaxed at their work place, share stories, have a talent show and ensuring their family are all involved.
(Corporaterewards.com.uk-advantages-of-employee-retention)

How to use employment incentive programme to retain staff:

The most exciting way to keep staff fully motivated and productive is to recognise their achievements and to reward for their efforts. When an employee has been recognised for their well performed task, getting a reward make the employee feel wanted and appreciated for what job they have been assign to do. Employees are the number one asset in your company which makes it very important to ensure they stay happy without any problems. This will enhance the productivity of the employee working at your establishments, speed and accuracy will be doubled, motivation will be increased and other employee would like a piece of the pie as well. When an employee understands that working better and hard will eventually get their rewards, then by putting in the effort employees are eventually would be recognised for their effort.

The incentive programme to retain staff has many ways ensure the staff remain and there are several ways of doing it. Below is the example of ways to improve staff morale and their loyalty to remain.

- Employee of the Month (added bonus into their salary)
- Recognition of exemplary staff (added bonus into their salary)
- Increment of salary
- Promoting the employee (when an employee has good recognition)
- Employee's Party (every 3 months once)
- Management trainee programme
- Trainings (can be outside to establishment or state)
- Holiday packages with family
- Birthday Parties (together with families)
- Employee benefits
- Commission basis (when they recommend a customer to the business)

These benefits will ensure that the employee will remain loyal and confident towards their employer, thus to ensure that the employee recognised their employer and respect them accordingly. (Corporaterewards.com.uk-advantages-of-employee-retention)

The bottom-line results:

The most important in committeemen is to improve on the bottom-line results, experience and committeemen staff usually makes decision which is beneficial to themselves, their colleagues and to their company. In the collaboration with projects, this committeemen staff ensure the progress of the projects without problems, mitigating issues pertaining to decision making and improving on productivity and performance. Retaining all your top employees ensure the knowledge of the company is high and able to save expenses on high employee turnover. Investing on existing staff will boost the company performance and the profits which is very important to every employee and employer of the establishments. (smallbusiness.chron.com/effects-team-commitment)

Connect with you staff:

The only best way to be closer and connected with your staff is by proper communication and always clearing the air and repeating your information. Not everyone receive the information correctly, hence you have to make it your duty to always communicate with them daily, call for a management briefing, call the head of department and supervisor, share ideas through solid input, connect with them, listen to their problem in the work place, how to effectively find solution to a problem and guide them the proper way of finding a solution is to communicate effective amongst their peers and be patient. (grapevinesurveys.com/blog/why-employee-loyalty-is-important)

When connecting with your employee you not only get their attention, you can effectively hear their voice and feel their emotion. It is so important to explore variety in communication skills; a very good example is a group chat such as "WhatsApp messaging" or other social media messaging which stores messages and keep everyone up to date with any latest information. In the hospitality industry there will be "one" social media messaging amongst their management team, and several other social media messaging for various department where messages are just related by "Copy and Paste", everyone gets a piece of the pie.

The other method of communication is by company email where connected to mobile phones is, hence the disadvantage is that a very good "Internet Wi-Fi Network" has to be installed and same goes to the social media chat. The other way of communication is putting up a "Bulletin Board" in the staff cafeteria where everyone gets a piece of the pie as well, it is a slow process yet "old school" method but information is passed down generally.

To provide a reason for your employees to be loyal:

Do not aspect your employee to just get a free hand of loyalty, they have to earn that loyalty and by doing this is ensuring they must get the message that the employer cares for the employees by word of mouth, engaging with the employees and allowing them to tell good things about the employer, having a stress free working environment, having good communication, gaining their trust by the employers coming down and helping them and having a conversation and the most important of all is to ask about their family.
(grapevinesurveys.com/blog/why-employee-loyalty-is-important)

Talking about employee family is not a small issue, it brings a satisfaction to the employee that the employer is concern on their well-being, having an employee and family get together is one of the most important co-curriculum activities a company should have. Is not about a "Budget" which a company should have, it is about the humanity concern of a family which are safe and happy, an unsatisfied family may cause stress and poor productise of an employee. The matter is not about paying off their loan or solving his personal problem but is to let them know you are there for them emotionally and in strength, having concern on our employee welfare such as their birthday and children birthday is one way of showing comfort to say your family is my family. Looking thoroughly into employee welfare, if an employer look at the benefits of employee welfare, in return the employee will surely generate a sense of loyalty towards the employer, that why a very good Human Resource is needed to organise the employee database as their names, date of birth, how many kids they have, children date of birth and their spouse information. A simple thing as a cake, present or monthly employee's children birthday bash is always good where their father and mother can always join and celebrate, having this will definitely create a very big loyalty towards the employer, small gestures goes a very long way.

Playing your role perfectly:

No matter how close you are as an employer whom connects with the employees, always remember you are the "Boss", the employee's needs to depend on your decision making, even in a tight space the employees look at you as their leader, without your decision the employees will not move. The employee must have faith and trust in you when making a decision and always hearing their thought may give you a better way of finding solution, they are the ones who are always with the guest and they communicate with the guest every day, their input is to be taken seriously. Once you are able to make a split-second decision, the employer have eventually won their heart, trust and loyalty.

Showing your support to them is very important, showing yourself as an employer and a team player have its advantages, mingling with them while working closely allows them a sense of relieve that the employers understand their job task and role. It is not wrong for an employer to pick up a dirty linen or a dirty plate, "hand must be dirty" in some occasion to show your connection and job role with the employees.

Being a good example towards your employee:

Bring a loyal employer has its huge advantages where employer is able to learn from the employers many trade skills. A loyal employer always gets full support from the employees where passion and potential both co-exist due to the felling of trust and being there for the employees. The other more exact way of being loyal to your employees is to have a very good benefit program and to be a role model to them, they are many ways of being a role model which is being the for them and teaching them how to improve themselves. The expression "leaders are made not born", one most essential attribute that a leader must have is showing by example, guiding the employee and the efficient way to manage certain work management ethics. Being a role model is that you are always under the magnifying glass and always been observed by your employees, they will always come to you for guidance and instruction when they are lost.

Sources retrieve from:

(grapevinesurveys.com/blog/why-employee-loyalty-is-important)
(contractormag.com/columns/broudy/role-model-employees-0310)

CHAPTER 7

Will the use of Tonality in communication writing improved business?

Vocal tone is extremely important where it tell a person about who you are, what you have and of your profession. Voice tone will either repel others or get the attention of other if the tonality is correct and way of communication has an important message. Short talks usually do not give appropriate information where it is just a conversation without a topic or agenda, is just an open topic of what a person think and express. A better understanding of tone, you are able to adjust the volume of your tone, adjust your pitch and frequency where your voice will have the right way to communicate effectively. By using the right way of communicating and using the right tonality, a business in way of marketing will eventually pick up and increase in profitability and customers.
(Maria Pellicano, March 18, 2018)

A well maintain management needs to look after all working voice in their establishments, they don't only improve on customers satisfaction and customers loyalty, but the management has to also retain them from leaving the company by effectively handing them great benefits and training by external parties where this will surely boost their communication skills. Working voices are those will valuable knowledge of the operations, products and the enable to sell a product using their voice and language for communication. In all job listing which we receive or see on the internet requires a very good communication skills, standing at a corner or your bakery will not sell anything, only passing client will just watch and there is no information being distributed towards them, yet no food tasting sample are being distributed. Even a bakery can be done in your own home yet if there is no proper communication between your clients or proper information been utilised by using social media or telemarketing, there is no way a product can be sold, it can be only be eaten by our own family member and we will lose our cost and budget. Effective communication is crucial and without its company and employee is will not function properly and to show any profits, managing the communication is the most essential way in any business even selling a simple menu or snacks. Many marketers have problem with effective of using communication, poor communication can cause many issues in a business, when communication information are passed on wrongly at the wrong time or place, productivity in the workplace can go down causing an effect which effects the employees of the establishment even their morale. (Pavel Aramyam, Oct8, 2015)

On the other hand, an effective communication can have a beneficial effect towards their employee where this will improve on employee morale, better retention rate and their overall productivity or dedication towards the company. In this chapter will be explain five ways on effectively improving communication and improvement of its business profitability's. The five-essential way of improving business will be expressed and define on the accountability of each action which will improve the business.

Less Misunderstanding:

When information which is not passed onto people correctly, may perception or misunderstanding tend to materialise which will affect the performance and the productivity off the company and the emotional effects of the employees. Personal agenda will submerge by unsatisfied employee towards their peers. This severe case can have a downfall effect on the company when a subject of the misunderstanding is not solving hence cause the employer and the company to lose capital and profits which would affect their month quota and budget. When there is a lack of communication, confusion arises by all employees. Many employees will assume the management has given instruction to them but another employee has misinterpreted the information wrongly, which may cause many confusions in any establishment, fights seldom occurs which loses the productivity momentum in an organization.
(Pavel Aramyam, Oct8, 2015)

Empowerment and Transparency:

Empowerment is a very productive and a high motivational tool where employers has the proper instruction and information which are passed down to their employee which productivity are risen and committeemen are enhance due to the employees feel confident with the information given. The instruction is repeated meticulously without hesitation by the management or not employer.

Employee who has more information given to them are more committed with their job which makes them more committed to complete the task due to a responsibility and trust towards the employer. Communication create a bond of culture, a family-oriented feeling in the organization which enables them to coordinate and perform even better.
(Pavel Aramyam, Oct8, 2015)

Healthy Culture:

An effective communication is gain by a very professional, healthy and productive cultures, when managers and employees have a very good relationship in the workplace, the communication between them will be a smooth flow without any hesitation to flaw.

The transparency of a healthy culture is to not misunderstand but to repeat an instructed communication wisely with the proper tonality in communication, every employee has a different EGO, and we ought to choose the right word not to trigger that EGO in order for the employee to understand what happens between employer, management and employee.
(Pavel Aramyam, Oct8, 2015)

Increase Accountability:

When the art of good communication is presented properly towards all employee, the employee feels the responsibility to be accountable for their task which makes the committeemen and delivery of their task impeccable. When a very clear instruction is given, workers know what to aspect from each other and the commitment given to commit and to finalise their task. Accountability refers to a sense of responsibility which management and employers look into every employee, without accountability there will be no rewards, incentive or promotion.
(Pavel Aramyam, Oct8, 2015)

Clear Direction:

The purpose of a clear communication is the get from the employer to the employee a clear direction towards where there are heading to, how to bring the company towards a high profitability, high productivity and to get highly motivated. A clear sense of direction is the most valuable in any communication between employees and employer. How the future will be developed is by a clear communication between the employees from the employer, it is also good habit for the employer to understand communication very well, employing a management employee with a "Mass Communication" or attending some communication course will be an added advantage for the establishments. When the employer understands the power of communication and adapt the knowledge with the precise tonality in communication will enhance the moral and allow the communication to pass through smoothly without any problem, such problem will only occur when the art of communication is not strong and also between the employees. It is important for the management to select semi management position such as "Supervisor" who has good communication skills which allows them to be a bridge between the rank and file and the management.

Giving an exact instruction to your employees gives a sense of confidence and motivation because they understand every work the employer says and always a good habit to repeat each instruct with an appropriate tonality and frequency without triggering a bad emotion by your employees. The company should adhere more on utilizing good communication skills because it will increase good productivity and the fundamental ways of working completely with s team of committed employees. Numerous establishments imagine that establishing a good communication inside a company will be expensive, here are way to mitigate the extensive expensive and increase productivity in your company.

Newsletter:

Once of the ways to utilize a newsletter is to allow internal employees to read the newsletter where is good to have a game with it such as "pop quiz", "reading competition" and "fun reading" meaning news pertaining to employees jokes or story where the newsletter should be printed and setup once every month. Employee would have fun while laughing with internal jokes such as "Mr ABC" was making coffee and accidentally dirties his uniform's" with a picture with it. Having picture amongst co-workers is simple to get by due to the heavy usage of "social media". (Pavel Aramyam, Oct8, 2015)

Secondly, this newsletter should list all the achievement of the employees on what they have contributed to achieve a high profitability, every successful project is to be listen where it is important to have a simple journalism to contribute what he has seen and what the company has seen in the company to achieve success. Noticing the performance of the employees and their career is a very good effort to increase their moral and by reading to improve their communication skills. Employee always will request their colleagues to explain certain phrase or sentence which they do not understand which actually increase their skills of communications.

Intranet:

Many companies do not fully utilize the intranet where it is specifically useful for exchanging information internally between the employees. Company intranet can create two-sided information of exchange such as business video campaign, news, jokes, planned marketing efforts, ideas by the employees and also tips on how to increase productivity and to be a management employee.
(Pavel Aramyam, Oct8, 2015)

Face to face:

Nothing is more effective than a confrontation between employees face to face such as greeting them, giving a pad on the back and smiling at them. It is also valuable to share jokes with them to increase the motivational and productivity knowing that the employer is closer to the employees. It is also important when going face to face it is necessary to allow your employees to still know and

understand you are the boss. Chatting with the employees is also a number priority where discussing with certain issues and problem may get an extensive idea to find a solution of a problem.
(Pavel Aramyam, Oct8, 2015)

Process of analysing problem and how to communicate efficiently by (Sharmadas Senasi)

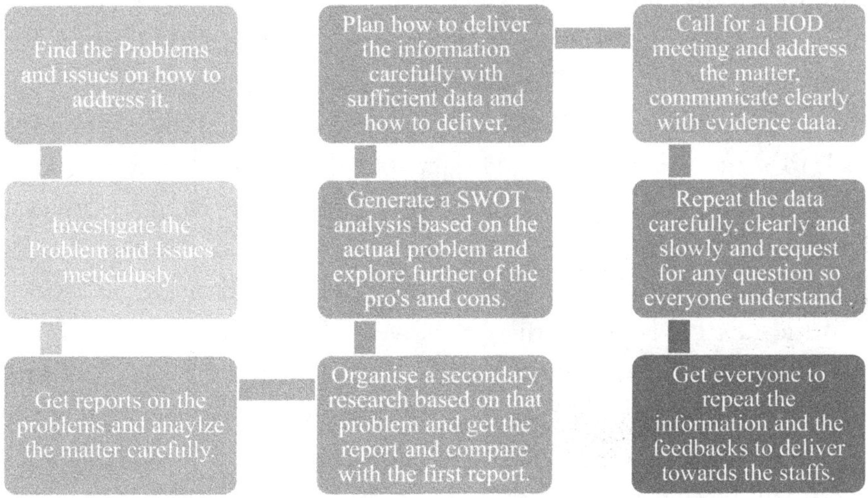

This explain the process of analysing a problem and how to communicate with all employee carefully using the step which states the breakdown of procedure and how to get the correct and sufficient data. This also allows the employer to get relevant data and a secondary data without losing valuable data before delivery of the solutions. Hence, by cultivating a SWOT analysis, it brings to the employer relevant information and facts on how to deliver a correct and clear information and data to all employees.

The tonality and its importance in business communication:

Written communication is different from the way we communicate and how we listen especially in a business-oriented position. Written communication has room for changes, deliberation, correction and review which can be adjusted or revised where else communication cannot be revised or corrected, once you communicate wrongly, harm has been done where there is no room for correction, emotional injury has been done. The art of tone and language are confusing things to deal when it comes to the way of communication, when you talk to someone, their eye contact, paralanguage, body language, intonations, pitch and voice give you clues about what is a person feeling. In a written communication there is no such area of body language and there is non-verbal signal for interaction, once a written communication is given, there is no retrieving back.

When in writing, the tone is actually defined as the writer attitude towards the writer and how they express themselves through words and the overall tone effects the readers emotionally which makes them feel happy, sad, afraid or threaten.

(universalclass.com/articles/writing/business-writing/appropriate-tone-in-business)

Writing a right tone for a document depends on the ability of the writer to understand the reader feeling and able to fine tune in order for the reader to understand and react to the documents.

Example of three way of writing communication tone:

- **You will have to finish this work, failure of not completing it will result in a "show cause" letter towards you.**

- **A "show cause" letter will be given to you if you do not complete the task given to you.**
- **Please finish this work in order for us to get the contract, if you need any assistance kindly asked from the management; hence this work is given to you because of the trust of the management towards you knowing you will be the right person for the job.**

Above are the example of written communication tone, each sentence reacts differently which threaten the individual as a forceful way of completing which is not suitable, the reader which is doing the job will not be able to focus due to the written warning if the individual does not complete it.

The last written communication mostly gives a motivation or faith towards the individual that they are able to source assistance from the management and able to be fully motivated due to the confidence which is given towards the individual.

Tone in communication can alter many emotions and some does because personal emotional harm as you can see from the communication tone which have listen in the example, readers may get emotional and this may also lose focus on their task and may jeopardise the work. When conveying an important tone in a negative manner, it will make the situation more difficult for the reader to accept. The communication tone such as jealousy, anger and frustration have to be avoided in the usage of communication tone, and this negativity is easily intercepted by the reader and emotionally interrupt their focus on their career.

Tone is a remarkable way of written communication for readers to read but even with good intention it can be interpret it wrongly which cause an emotional harm, the best mantra is to revise, revise and to revised your documentation before sending it, it is always good to have your business partner to go through again and again to ensure the message is correct and will do no emotional hard to the reader, that why editors are important, even in the newspaper firms there is always multiple editor to go through a hot story.

It is best to avoid working which sound insincere which will cause too many judgement and assumption, and avoid the use of jargon language which many jargon languages seem to have many meaning it, using industrial language will make reader confused and judgmental. Have more statistical numbers so reader can see, also to explain what the number mean in order to get the reader attention and to ensure they understand what it means. Panting a clarify picture of the statistical review ensure the full commitment of the reader to go through and it is not just an art, ensure to explain the detailed. The other end is to always say why and explain the reason so reader may not come into a conclusion; hence giving another judgmental false review which leads to misconception. (universalclass.com/articles/writing/business-writing/appropriate-tone-in-business)

In communicating with your audience through written business communication, there are two factors we have to look at which is "what you say" and "how you say it", even the most basic communication can be presented wrongly through the use of wrong tonality. Look at business relationship or at home, how often we get into an argument just because we use the wrong tonality and the wrong sentence, even in the office if we were to send a message to our colleague with a wrong sentence it may get emotional or dramatically abusive.

(Printward staff, Aug 22, 2012- The importance of tone in business writing-and how to use it)

Conveying a tone is pretty much simple where you can yell, scream, and speak sarcastically but trying to convey a message through written communication is not easy since we do not have time on our side to get our point directly across. There are there basic fundamental tones which is needed and can be used in writing with several factors, these three are the most basic in communication writing which enables you or giving you a guideline on the ways to communicate in written effectively with mitigating problems. Below are the three important tools which is needed to write a written communication effectively.

- **Audience**
- **Message**
- **Medium**

Audience:

Tailor your tone to speciality suite the audience you are looking for, target audience is the most effective way in selecting your written communication. By targeting your audience or performing a feasible study in way of performing a full "SWOT" you are able to identify the range of ages, the slang on using for your communication, whether to add humour and what important information based on the branding. Identifying your audience is your number one priority in presenting a written communication, a survey needs to be done in order to identify the way of communication.
(Printward staff, Aug 22, 2012- The importance of tone in business writing-and how to use it)

E.g.: If you have created a special sweet dessert menu in your hotel, the way of presenting a written communication has to be sharp, sweet, identifying your customers and using the appropriate slang to be used to gather their attention. There is no point just writing a basic communication using lame old terms and boring quotes where certain "target market" will only glance through. Your target audience needs to be the young generation who has a "sweet tooth" where you will know getting their attention is easier.

Message:

Think about the actual content of the message which you trying to put and this message has to be based on the product you are promoting, without a product it impossible to write the message,

based on the product experience you have had, it will be easier for you to write. You have seen the product, tasted and experience the products, then promoting the product you need to use electrifying words which give an attention towards the products.
(Printward staff, Aug 22, 2012- The importance of tone in business writing-and how to use it)

E.g.: Going back to the sweet dessert menu, the words has to be expressed when you are trying out the menu, the emotional response you get by tasting the product is the way you feel the message going through and emotionally expressing yourself on the taste, flavour and presentation. It is important to get the Chef to give some words of preparation which is important to the readers as well, this will give an in-depth look into the products.

Medium:

To select the appropriate medium to which you have to select your option to where the message will be going, is it on a newspaper, social media's, emails or billboards. Target the best way in getting your clients, selecting the social Media's and newspapers are the best way to capture your markets.
(Printward staff, Aug 22, 2012- The importance of tone in business writing-and how to use it)

E.g.:
When getting youth attention to try your menu, is always great to go through the social media where young generation prefers the internet.

These three factors create a standard blueprint for you where you may enhance the ability more towards other area which you may try. These guidelines effectively create a way to properly prepare a written communication where you are able to reach in a macro communication. The tone you use in written communication give you a personality where readers can identify the emotional attachment in those written words, phrases and sentence used may get the reader attached and able to feel what you are writing, there personality will enable you have a brand where customers can identify you and getting emotional attached to your products. When your brand is good, many customers will stick with you eventually, trying out all the product you have to offer, basically in a layman's term, is a fan club. Establishing a unique type a tone will enable you to create a brand where if you have a strong brand identity, it can be converted into a copyright where you can plan what you want to have the branding involved, it can be a very unique quote of brand based on your products. Once you have fully understand your brand, then the next phase it to create a character for your brand by taking the qualities of the brand and turning into something majestic which embodies your brand, the brand you choose, the character and the qualities have to have a similarities which brings to one possible conclusion, the identity of your branding where people are mesmerised like "Mark's and Spencer's".

(Printward staff, Aug 22, 2012- The importance of tone in business writing-and how to use it)

The most easiest and common way to have a written tone is to have a very good branding which have been marketed well, strong branding is determine by the type of customers you have, type of marketing you have done, the quality of the products and the quality of the written tone which helps to advertise it.

According to "Purdue University Online Lab", a tone writing is a part of the writer's attitude, their emotions which is covered with their words where the tone effects the reader's emotional response. (Inside Business-The Hampton Road Business Journal 2012, 15 June)

In business writing in communication, the writer has to match the tone of the message and to ensure that the message have a chain reaction towards the message written. There are four important question which a person should ask themselves before writing a business communication.

- What is the main purpose of the communication?
- Who is the target audience we are looking for?

- What should the audience learn from our message and their understanding?
- What type of action should the audience take after reading the message?

How we present a message is just as important as the message itself, we do not want to go outside of the chapter, keeping in touch with the message and to allow ourselves to explore more possibilities is important. In writing a formal communication between your subordinates has to be clear of the intention where we have to identify they are in a different level and much more senior, using the correct written tone is important, also to remember that a written tone may represent itself into a different meaning if the message is not explain well. The written communication has to have the purpose of the message where keep straight to the point will be the absolute importance, where else writing to your peers will not necessarily need to be formal.

There are three main ways to effectively communicate in business which is verbal, non-verbal and written. All of these three main areas are important in successfully up selling a product of your establishments. No matter what level of hierarchy you are at, writing skills communication is an asset for many establishments, it is the ground work for making a product successful and making a brand of it. The list of written communication is long where is goes from letter writing, newsletters, company brochure, social media updates, visual aids, presentation slides, case studies and other related company document. These are the written document will be changing the status of your business where people will start to hear about on the products which you have. The way we write and boost our career or hamper our work for the beneficial of the company, in the globalization era of the 21st century, many generation "X" and "Y" are using the internet platform for mass marketing, macro and micro seems to be very small because of the instant connectivity of the internet. Businesses now advertise many in the internet where most of their major population are internet savvy, the use of the internet gets the message across very fast without delays.

(10 reason why business writing is so important- Dec, 6, 2017, Michelle Brooks)

There are ten huge benefits in why business writing is so important in any industries. Below are the ten important findings.

1. ***A writing skill ensure an effective business communication.***

A business correspondence is an important tool which keeps your owner and stakeholder up to date information, to ensure the written communication is clear and goes straight to the point. Meticulous writing skills in written communication is important in order for the readers understand the information and also state why with a validated information.

If the text written is poor, it will be difficult for the reader to digest the information arising to many questions which puts your position in harm's way; hence effecting your career for the future. (10 reason why business writing is so important- Dec, 6, 2017, Michelle Brooks)

2. ***A writing skill makes the different between good and bad.***

Writing a business communication for marketing or report with bad grammatical errors will definitely put you on the leash where career wise will be affected. This bring bad judgement upon yourself, always prove read your information and ask for a second opinion to go through it properly. Writing with a bad sentence or grammatical error allows people to judge you easily and this will not be ignored by the management or company, your skills will be question whether are you appropriate for the job and task given to you.
(10 reason why business writing is so important- Dec, 6, 2017, Michelle Brooks)

3. ***Demonstrate your intelligence.***

Trying to avoid grammatical errors will ensure you are writing a good marketing advertisement, having to make a wrong grammatical error may allow other people to judge you as unintelligent, ensure reading a lot of news article and newspaper will allow you to adapt and mitigate flaws in your writing skills.
(10 reason why business writing is so important- Dec, 6, 2017, Michelle Brooks)

4. ***A good writer is credible.***

Senders whom send good writing skills are reliable and trustworthy person, their ability to prove read and creating good sentences are always considered intelligent. Try to imagine yourself receiving a marketing newsletter which has wrong abbreviation and spelling mistakes, what will we think about the sender. Emphasize on others and ensure we always go through our work before sending it to avoid embarrassment. A good competent writer always proofread to avoid any mistakes which effects their credibility or branding, an incompetent writer never proofread and cause grammatical error which loses many credibility in an establishment which eventually effect their career in the long run.
(10reason why business writing is so important- Dec, 6, 2017, Michelle Brooks)

5. ***Be more influential.***

If you have a good persuasion skill will be beneficial wherein allows you to influence other to achieve your goals, a persuasive skill enable your reader to understand and grasp what you have written and allow themselves to explore the product which is been promoted.
(10 reason why business writing is so important- Dec, 6, 2017, Michelle Brooks)

If you are describing a new product to your board of director, your written communication skills need to be convincing where they feel the product, understand the nature and purpose of the products and have a vote of confidence that the product is able to sell and to gain profit. The major word in using in promoting a new product is the profitability where you have a very convincing demographic study of your area.

6. ***The Business writing convey courtesy.***

The written communication of business portrays the same level of politeness and humbleness as we do communicate when face to face towards our superiors. The courtesy business writing letters actually express the writer's feeling and emotion towards the reader where the readers feel the emotional connectivity of the writer. The reader can then understand the content of the message, the feeling imbedded in the message while reading, even they may acknowledge the professionalism from the company branding that the writers express the full product knowledge of the company.
(10 reason why business writing is so important- Dec, 6, 2017, Michelle Brooks)

This is also important for "Executive Chef" and Food and Beverage Managers" where they strive to collaborate with menu writing skills, menu writing skills is as important as business communication where the creator of the menu and the writer of the food products explain thoroughly of the menu, quality, taste and the essence in creating such menu. The menu writing explains the synopsis of the flavour, texture, food culture, preparation complex and the elegance of the menu. Readers then may feel the passion, emotional feeling of the menu product so readers may picture it.

7. ***A writing skill helps to keep record.***

Oral communication does not last for long where their records cannot be kept or saves, how we human connects through centuries years of history is through the usage of book where scholars has kept record of history, these records will last long and can be used as references.
(10 reason why business writing is so important- Dec, 6, 2017, Michelle Brooks)

Keeping and storing in hard copy is the best solution where is can be retrieve back after many years, this record is essential in any business association, in Malaysia currently all taxation report and income tax are kept for 8 years till is no longer needed.

Any reports we do or create is best to keep in record and store it appropriately according to dates, months and years, this record assist us in keeping tract on past and present logs.

8. ***Boosting your professional confidence.***

Any writing is important, we write proposal to gather interested investors, we create report to show to our management, we create dissertation to prove our findings, we generate a business writing proposal to get loan to be invested, the more we write up we gain experience and confidence. (10 reason why business writing is so important- Dec, 6, 2017, Michelle Brooks)

Once a confidence has been established, business writing skills will be easier as we have identified the correct correspondent language and the criteria in writing. Confidence is gained by nurturing our writing skills, the more we make mistake is easier for us to learn from our superiors where they will mentor and guide us the correct path to success. Writing a proposal there is no format, it only needs experience on what subject and subtext needed to establish a format.

9. ***Self-promoting and enhancing your career.***

When you are good in written communication skills, many of your colleague will always come around you to get advice and to check their work or edit them. This normally takes a vote of confidence by your co-worker, normally words do go around till the management hears of this. This portrays a vote of confidence in the management book where assisting and guiding others in your skill management programmes.
(10 reason why business writing is so important- Dec, 6, 2017, Michelle Brooks)

When top management need someone to draft and important email or document, they will surely turn to you because of the confidence level they see in you and the word of mouth which all employee is talking good thing about you. All the employee will always point their hand at you when asked who the best writer is. Management and employer will certainly entrust a new position to enhance your career by retaining you and putting in a programme for career enhancement.

10. ***A business write-up creates a strong web presence.***

A business is all about creating a presentation, this presentation creates a presence in the website, it has to be strong and full of information. Great business critter always affiliates their work with the business prospect and products. The nature for the presence of the website is to allow potential clients and investor to know your company and understand its mission and vision. Product are important in creating an awareness of what the company is about.

(10 reason why business writing is so important- Dec, 6, 2017, Michelle Brooks)

To attain this goal, the company creates blogs, newsletters and social media's account where the website may be link to it. The quality of the content must be strong and important, business writer who is able to sell products through the website is considered very strong because of the usage of business writing communications.

Effective communication which leads to business growth:

Learning how to effectively communicate well by choose the right word, tone and frequency will indicate how well verse you are and the benefit of increase your business growth. As an employer, communicating with them with small success and sharing with them the effectiveness of this is a key success for a business, employee will then understand and learn to adapt and improve on their communication skills. Communicating with them with the success of profit allows the employees to be more confident of the company which allows them to be more confident and will improve their key performance index (KPI). Being an employee and learning how to communicate effectively will make you an interest for the company and will increase the value in the company and the market place.
(Good communication skills will help you find long-term success, Entrepreneur, Nov 7,2014, Byju Raveendran)

There are three way in mastering the skills of communication that can improve your business and to increase your success rate.

1. ***Expanding the reach of your market place.***

Knowing your business mission, vision, services and mission statement without the proper communication skill will not improve your business and company growth, it is essential to understand and master the communication skills, one single wrong phrase or statement will not allow you to grow the business and you cannot recall back the phrase or word which has been communicated.

(Good communication skills will help you find long-term success, Entrepreneur, Nov 7, 2014, Byju Raveendran)

It is always good to plan and write up important words that would increase your chances to improve marketing your business and using the correct words will mitigate the boosting of your company.

Ensure when communicated, the right tonality, right message and right frequency is being used to get attention from your market, if you are to snobbish it will be difficult for you to reach your market, if you do not have experience in communication well it will be an downfall for the company; hence, the employees of your company will not support you. Giving the full support to your employees and making them understand that communication is the essence of connecting reputable client and benefiting from their support and loyalty.

2. ***To lead and educate.***

Showing leadership skills towards your employee will be a great beneficial towards your company, employee who seeks job employment always interested to learn new trade, new skills and how to improve themselves. Education is part of the new concept for the industry where they may learn and gain knowledge on how to be more active in their job.

E.g.: In Malaysia HRDF or known as "Human Resource Division Funds" are claimable where employers are urge to register with the this government affiliated agency where any out-sourcing company which gives training with a valid "Certified Trainer" and registered with HRDF as a trainer, the organisation can pay and claim back directly from HRDF. This cope of funds which is made availability by the government urges employer to use this platform to train employees. Another example of an existing company which does training for Hotels and other business is "I-HR" located in Malaysia and the Chief executive Officer "Mr. Roy Prasad" lead the team to increase the knowledge of employer and employees. His company is legally registered with "HRDF".

3. ***Ability to motivate.***

The most valuable aspect in mastering the skills of written communication or verbal communication is the ability to inspire, the word inspire is strong yet powerful enough to make dreams comes through, this phrase has to be used daily where this art has the capabilities to increase the positivity of a person personality and attitude and ensuring their perform to their best of their abilities. Finding the time to lead, guide, inspire and motivating your employees to see pass the roadblock and how to find valuable solution and the patients to create something new.

To improve sales and profitability, written communication is essential to sales representative, they need to be proficient in reading and writing skills. These skills are valuable to the front-line staff where it is crucial for them to understand and take up these skills. There are seven important skills for them to understand and use this method to improve the productivity of sales.
(Michele Mcgovern-7 writing skills you will need to please customers)

4. ***Critical reading.***

Written communication does not come with much explanation and it is important for the readers understand the correct way of reading and identifying vital information for them to understand. Training the eyes to be meticulous is essential for the business where this will aid you in identifying important phrases and key words.

In a company, reading emails or text message through social media is essential for understanding, not much information is being explain, only important phrases and keywords are written down. So, email or text message will have short meaning and short hand where only the writer understand, the reader have to identify this meaning and communicate back to the writer to confirm the meaning and definition.
(Michele Mcgovern-7 writing skills you will need to please customers)

5. *Time management*

Often sales managers while having a conversation with their client, it is always to step away from the conversation to reciprocal all information and process it carefully. Too much conversation will allow important key notes and information to be forgotten, it is advisable to always excuse yourself and process and think of a solution rather than having a conversation while thinking of a solution, this brings to your attention that you would be busy thinking of a solution at the same time not concentrating with other conversation.
(Michele Mcgovern-7 writing skills you will need to please customers)

6. *The effectiveness of questioning.*

It will be a good habit to ask question when reading an email or reading a text, this will explain more on topics which needs more understanding. Enabling the question will adhere more understanding and clearing the air will make both parties understand will getting the general idea and solution towards a problem. Exchange of emails and text message is not only important but getting a frequent asked question is more important, the issue of getting the benefit of the doubt is in questioned, understanding the message and planning your question is more vital in getting the right message rather than assumptions.

When question is not asked correctly, then the listener or the reader will not get the full fact of information, mistakes are generated based on assumption that they understood, is better to clarify the questions in order to benefit the right message rather than creating mistakes and rectifying it which gives a bad judgement of yourself.
(Michele Mcgovern-7 writing skills you will need to please customers)

Empathy.

It is always challenging to express emotion onto written communication unless you have identified the person or the team you are writing to, is also important to use a written tone which make the reader feel calm and understand your information. It is also important to acknowledge the person with positive words to ensure they are comfortable with you, give remarkable gesture like "well done", "I am sure you are right" or "I know you are correct", this will bring a sense of loyalty as well as humbleness from them. (Michele Mcgovern-7 writing skills you will need to please customers)

Humility.

Professional can build a good credibility with their client is by not telling them that you know all the facts and admitting that you need to check and confirmed the message properly. When a discussion has commenced and needed the representative to solve it and knowing that the information is correct, is always a must to collaborating it by investigating and getting to know the correct information before communicating it. Let your customer know by telling them, "Please give me 5 to 10 minutes for me to confirmed the correct information, it will take a few minutes and I hope you don't mind waiting so I may give you the answer". By giving them this assurance, your customer will feel oblige and satisfies with your investigation.
(Michele Mcgovern-7 writing skills you will need to please customers)

Adaptability.

Customers will always write to the representative on comment and question they think will wisely be used in the industry, the representative ought to create a standard answer where it would satisfy the customers at the same time this will ensure the standard answered is been given to other customers as well.

Create a standard answer such as *"Okay, will surely look into it", or "Okay, thank you for your input" or "Okay, thank you for your valuable insights".*

A standard template response will be important in the industry where there is no justification needed or to explain the reason, this

standard template answers will acknowledge our customers and ensure their comment or question has been answered.
(Michele Mcgovern-7 writing skills you will need to please customers)

Grammar and Spelling and their importance.

Any written letter such as email or in the social media has to be taken seriously, spelling and grammar has to be taken into attention that clear exchange of information has to be precise and accurate in order for the reader to understand, sometimes short hand can cause many confused assumption where is not taken seriously when writing. The key point is to always ensure to always write well with good punctuation and ensure to always read back a letter you have written before sending it. Other reader may comment at your written with positive or negative feedback which put your skill and your benchmark into questions. Your branding is your personally trade, this brings to your professionalism in the business world, readers will judge your work base on your writing. An article depicts the emotion of the writer where readers may feel what you are writing based on the choice of word you use.
(Michele Mcgovern-7 writing skills you will need to please customers)

CHAPTER 8

Customers satisfaction intend to spend more

When it comes to satisfied customer, we can see that the customer just got an awesome deal where he is in fact satisfied and happy for the result he has been waiting for. The look on a satisfied customer is just like looking at a child after receiving his lollypop, the feeling of accomplishment. (Principle of Marketing- M Library Publishing)

A satisfied customer is defined when a product or services meet his expectation, the benchmark of his thirst for services which has been fulfilled, when their offering meet to their expectation, then it is clear to say that they are satisfied with the product and services which has been offered. Improving satisfaction is a daily task for all business establishment, it is a high demand expectation by customers, business people have to improve their customer satisfaction, companies may evaluate or conduct an appraisal towards your sales person based on the total customers satisfaction they have received. Sales person would be given a quota to hit their sales for a specific month, it is the duty of the sales person to create and executive a product reach out, a micro and macro analysis ought to be done to identify your market and try to research that particular point of interest to merge an interest of a product. There are many strategies to create customers satisfaction and to deliver them, here are 2 types which would assist in enabling to begin and focus on that particular delivery.

Establishing an appropriate expectation in the customers mind is very important, emphasising with them and understanding their wants and demand has to be done meticulously in order to create a proper benchmark and understanding their product desire. Establishing an expectation is important to determine how to understand your clients, that is why analysing your feasibility studies is important, identifying your potential market is very vital in setting up a foundation. A new products needs to be introduced, sampling is the most crucial of all, customer's needs to see for themselves, feel it, touch the product, or to taste a sample is always a good way where budget is to be planned on how much of samples you are needed to give out. The second way is to deliver the expectation to your customers, as a salesperson in a business establishment such as hotels, you would have created a database of your clients and they would be comfortable with you and have created a bonding of confidence. Creating and delivering an expectation is done by analysing your product and how to reach it out to people, having a road show at your establishment such in a hotel or office space is a good way to begin, this will enable you to generate a theme for a product which you would like to launch. Having support by your company and having your colleagues to back you up is one of the most crucial element in guest satisfaction, in satisfying a guest is always done with the team players in your group whom has striven to prepare brochures, journal, product manufacturing and the presentation of the products. Invitation with product sampling is a better way to deliver the customers expectation, such as BMW when the new 330e hybrid came into the market in Melaka, company ABC which lead my Mr. EDC, manage to gather his database of client such as Doctors, lawyers and professional consultant by inviting them to a special cocktail dinner and introducing the new BMW 330e. He has also managed to give a good trade in offer with existing BMW owners which he delivers their expectation to them which will increase their desire to purchase that car. His database of client would like to try out the new electric hybrid cars to experience the comfort and focus on lowering their petrol mileage. Once you have gathered all your clients, allow them to mingle amongst your team to feel the product, hold or to touch the product, emotionally feel the desire of having this product and to arrange for a test drive. Test drive is similar to a sampling of food where it emotionally takes to on a journey of taste and pleasure.

A dissatisfied customer will always tell more to their friends then a satisfied customer and their negative experience just to create a drama of expectations. In order to allow customers to tell their friends of a good experience, establishing an expectation of the mind towards your customer is pre-purchase communication where they will tell their friends where they have been and what discount was given and the service given. One of the best clients you will get is always entertaining women, their contact does go a long way, exchanging of food menu, experience and topic is always their daily bowl of salad. Understanding your clients is always knowing the desire in their heart, customers are more likely to promote your products and business when they are satisfied with the services which is offered to them. A good sales or a good deal or a good sales always gets the attention by your customers, you can rest assure that the biggest gossip around town will be your products where services are great, customers have to experience the first services given to them, again the word branding of your services and by your company is important. Having to wonder even a brushed up shop which look old that looks like 55 years old, having to serve a simple delicacy like pie's will always get the attention of favourite customers, not because the place looks old but it is because of the taste and the home service which is given by the owner. A satisfaction which is unexplainable because of the nobleness and humbles which comes together service a lovely pie, the unstoppable gossip which will goes round the town claiming as the best serving pie shop, word of mouth and social media would go all out just to find the Pie shop, a sweet delicacy where customer intend to spend more just to enjoy and experience the moment.

The most empowering moments of satisfying a guest is to have or conduct a program which is called "customer facing personnel", with this employee can then meet and interact with customers, Hotel Ritz Carlton practise this method to ensure the guest gets the fullest experience and satisfaction. Certain hotels or employees are given a budget to conduct activities from them ensuring their happiness. The employees are dependent on their years of services, experience, employee level and department, each budget is given a quota and an activity plan where report are made.
(Principle of Marketing- M Library Publishing)

In measuring customer satisfaction, we have to understand how to create it and how to deliver it, not only asking customer "were you satisfied" and companies are not asking the right question to attain a better prospective by their customer yet by asking the same question such as "how satisfied were you with our service", such question should not be copied. The question should be asked has to be meaningful and have to have a depth. To get customers review, such question should be driven into action in order to gain full detail of their experience. Such question consists of:

- Please define your satisfaction when our service is given?
- Which of our employees made your day and why?
- Was our product quality able to meet your expectation?
- If you were not happy with our service, kindly specify why?
- Would you recommend your family and friends here?

The other way in maintaining your sales figure is to have a free give away, everybody loves a free give away, and it will make sense to rewards your customers after they have spent a certain amount of cash in your business establishments. Your customers will certainly feel excited and happy once they have received a free parcel and to see something they have never expected. Giving something free does not mean your company will go bankrupt, a simple free gift which worth RM 10.00 to RM 20.00 would suffice, sometimes and company buys this free gift in a large amount usually gets a good deal from their supplier. Now many gifts are easily attained thru "Alibaba" and "Lazada" in large amount usually from China.

What will be the most ideal giveaway for them to have is the most expensive questions, but after several brain mapping we will often get the best answer. Cinema's now days are playing most of the latest movies such as Avengers, using this as a promotional character such as "Thor", "Ironman", "Hulk" and many more will be an exciting way to allow their children's to accompany their parents to have some fun, this way of promotion can be used in any businesses even in hotels.

Getting this Marvel character as a free gift is one of the best ideas in giving a free gift, kids would go insane in wanting a free gift, hence always asking their parents to buy more and to shop more. Spending an amount of RM 150 or more will surely urge a family to buy more just to get a free toy for their kids and this is the best way to allow customers to come to our establishments to spend more.

Nevertheless, offering a special bonus club for your clients is inviting more and more spenders to your business industry, adding a section on a part of a domain to get attention by clients who are really going through the website. Client would be proud taking out their special gold or platinum privilege card to be used to attained discount, off course many other clients would surely ask how to attain that special discount card. A membership card is the most important card in any business establishment and this allows customers to really understand what types of discount and services they will entitled. Looking at "Hotel ABC" and how they attain their customers is by telemarketing and selling their products and services. These particular hotels have many facilities and also entitles discounts, certain free meals or buffet, discounts on cake of the month, discount on Italian restaurant or coffee house, discount on SPA Massage, free stay in their hotel and discounts on beverages. Many members around Malaysia, one of the most successful membership attain program in Malaysia, the benefits of the membership is so successful where it is being utilised everyday with many business society, many business people are using this services and getting full benefits back. Their marketing strategy aims at working people by telemarketing services and a visit to the establishment to experience the services and the atmosphere of what is installed for them, nevertheless their closure period is fast where turnover of agreed customers is thrilled with the services offered by the hotel.

Corporate strategy has become important in customer satisfaction where increase customer satisfaction equal high profitability. According to Christian Homburg, Nicole Koschate, and Wayne. D (Do satisfied customers pay more) that recent notion found that there is an increase with customer satisfaction and financial performance. Another study which has an impact with increase profitability is by increase referral by existing customers by word of mouth.
(Mooradian and Olver 1997).

Customer satisfaction also effects the customers willingness to pay, pricing and profitability is an essential tool when costing is questioned, again if the product and branding is satisfaction by the management and proper questionnaires is done and presented, marketing is done impeccably well, surely pricing will not be an issue since a good part of marketing has been done for awareness.

(Christian Homburg, Nicole Koschate and Wayne D. Hoyer *Journal of Marketing* Vol. 69, No. 2 (Apr., 2005), pp. 84-96).
(e.g Finkelman 1993, Reichheld and sasser 1990).

Customers usually spend more when we identify potential spenders, such feasibility studies must be done to attained suitable candidates which also reflects on their current position of their careers, salary and live styles. Using the proper demographic tools, we will be able to gained information background with proper use of a questionnaires.

CHAPTER 9

Methodology

For the present study, questionnaire has been created speciality for the use of customers on their overall experience in the hospitality which involves how the information was received, the communication styles, and their nature of spending habits, what attracts them into our establishment. Using the same approach as "Yilmaz (2011)' I have currently taken samples questionnaires and modify it to suit the need of developing a questionnaire. The questionnaire was implemented on customers from various background which frequency visits hotel functions or goes for a meal in a 4 to 5-star hotel. The scope of this study was to analyze the effectiveness of Tonality in communication which can increase customer's satisfaction and improves profitability.

As below I have created a questionnaire based on "Yilmaz (2011") approach where I have modified the question by keeping it relevant "Yilmaz (2011)"

No	Statement questions	y	mb	n
1	Do you think the management needs to improve training to increase communication in productivity and sales?	92.2%	7.8%	

2	Does inter-department communication help employees to improve their language and communication skills?	82.4%	11.8%	5.8%
3	Do you think managements, should spend close attention to improve communication of employees on how to communicate with their customers?	92.2%	7.8%	
4	Should "Hotel Management" colleges improve their teaching and coaching on "Communication" skills in up-selling to a customer?	86.3%	11.8%	1.9%
5	Should employees take initiative to improve their communication habits and on how to start a conversation?	90.2%	7.8%	2%
6	As a buying customer, will you spend more when the services you received such as communication and information are to your expectations?	76.5%	17.6%	5.9%
7	As a customer while dining in a restaurant, will you spend more when the services you receive is exemplary such as food presentation knowledge, up-selling and taste quality of the food product?	72.5%	17.6%	9.8%
8	As a buying customer, do you acknowledge in proper marketing, product knowledge and up-selling through the use of good communication skills and tonality frequency being used towards you?	84.3%	7.8%	7.9%
9	As a customer, will you market the product quality and excellent services you have experience to your contacts?	82.4%	11.8%	5.8%
10	If you were an employee, do you think training and improving your skills continually will benefit you greatly?	94.1%	2.0%	3.9%

11	As an employee, will you be able to communicate when up-selling a product or services when proper training and guidance is given to you?	94.1%	5.9%	
12	Being an employee, will you be confident to up-sell and communicate effectively once you have experienced the products such as food and beverages.	88.2%	7.8%	3.9%
13	As an employee, do you believe without proper training in communication or products and services will affect the profitability of the establishments and your self-confidence?	84.3%	9.8%	5.9%
14	Do you think that hotel employees play a vital role in elevating our experiences and excitements?	86.3%	9.8%	3.9%
15	As a paying customer, the quality of product and services presented to you by the hotel employee has satisfied you greatly, will you return?	86.3%	5.9%	7.8%
16	As a customer, do you think proper communication of information given allows you to choose which variety of product or services to purchase more easily instead of getting the information by yourself?	88.2%	5.9%	5.9%
17	Do you think is worth the effort to support an establishment such as your favourite hotels or restaurants when remarkable service is been given equally to all customers?	84.3%	9.8%	5.9%
18	Do you think body language is important tool to be used when communicating your product and services?	86.3%	3.9%	9.8%
19	Once you have experienced a fruitful product and services of a hotel, will you recommend to your contacts of your best choice of hotel to be in?	92.2%	5.9%	2%

HYPHOTHESIS

Can communication improve customer's satisfaction in diverse ethnicity and improve profitability in the Hospitality Industry

In this hypothesis, a master survey has been created and was given to people who are in similar industries and a total number of 51 people have answered the survey. Evidently, there are 51 people who strongly believes towards communication and customer care do effectively and efficiently improve expectations and encourages spending. The survey question is attached in page 83 and 84, and the responded 51 people answers have been converted into a "pie chart" where their answers to the survey questions have been calculated into percentage. This will be in page 85 to 94 which has been attached and highlighted for the reader.

According to the survey, a majority of 90% have agreed that improvement of communication improves the profitability of the business organisation due to customer's satisfaction at the diners and hence improves familiarity and personal service to customers.

The purpose of the survey is to understand the reason for this research investigation towards this dissertation, understanding customer's perspective of their expectations in a hospitality or service industry. The information gathered by this survey will gather sufficient information on the improvement towards the hospitality and service industry. This research has also given inside towards achieving the improvement of communication and gaining the satisfaction, confidence and ensuring increase of profitability in the industry. It is also believed that without proper communications, achieving a customer's satisfaction and profitability will reduce the margin of customer's business spending and increases dissatisfaction through word of mouth or in social media.

REFERENCES

https://study.com/academy/lesson/communication-skills-in-the-hospitality-industry.html

https://www.ukessays.com/essays/communications/communication-in-the-hospitality-and-tourism-industry-communications-essay.php

http://ericksonian.com/tonality

https://www.pixus.uk/blog/the-importance-of-tone-of-voice-and-why-you-should-get-it-right/

https://www2.palomar.edu/anthro/language/language_6.htm

http://www.rightattitudes.com/2008/10/04/7-38-55-rule-personal-communication/

http://www.iojt-dc2013.org/~/media/Microsites/Files/IOJT/11042013-Albert-Mehrabian-Communication-Studies.ashx

http://www.abccopywriting.com/2010/08/31/tone-of-voice-brand

http://www.ethnicityonline.net/cross_cultural_communication.htm

http://bmjopen.bmj.com/content/6/3/e010042

https://www.wehoteliers.com/blog/communication-skills-hotel-industry/

http://blog.trainerswarehouse.com/communication-exercises/

https://www.fluentu.com/blog/educator-english/esl-listening-activities-intermediate/

https://benefitsbridge.unitedconcordia.com/top-7-health-benefits-smiling/

https://www.ncbi.nlm.nih.gov/pubmed/20432952

https://bestdentistsfortworth.com/smiling-boosts-your-immune-system/

https://www.zendesk.com/blog/right-tone-of-voice/

https://clubtraining.com.au/2013/06/20/hospitality-and-verbal-communication-go-hand-in-hand/

https://pilotscholars.up.edu/cgi/viewcontent.cgi?article=1089&context=cst_studpubs

https://clu-in.org/cihandbook/CIOCpage/croscultcomm.htm

https://www.forbes.com/sites/carolkinseygoman/2011/11/28/how-culture-controls-communication/#629d90a4263b

https://doctortyrone.wordpress.com/2008/08/15/the-3-barriers-to-effective-multicultural-communication-part-1/

https://journals.lww.com/academicmedicine/Abstract/2005/02000/Enhancing_Self_Awareness_in_Medical_Students__An.10.aspx https://doctortyrone.wordpress.com/2008/09/05/removing-the-barriers-to-effective-multicultural-communication-part-3/

https://www.ncbi.nlm.nih.gov/pmc/articles/PMC2805066/

http://successfully-speaking.com/blog/the-three-vs-of-communication

http://customersthatstick.com/blog/customer-service-techniques/communication-the-most-important-skill-in-customer-service/

smallbusiness.chron.com/impact-customer-service-customer-satisfaction-2087.html

smallbusiness.chron.com/impact-good-customer-service-small-business-2080.html

http://www.telephonedoctor.com/our_blog/how-improving-communication-skills-increases-bottom-line-results/

http://smallbusiness.chron.com/tonality-marketing-33557.html

file:///G:/DBA/reference%20article/Communication%20%20How%E2%80%99s%20Your%20Tone%20%20%E2%80%94%20Judy%20Jablon.html

bookboon.com/blog-effective communicationskills

Glenn Wilson-Body language

Fernandesbiodataofsuccess

https://hbr.org/2016/08/an-emotional-connection-matters-more-than-customer-satisfaction

https://hbr.org/2015/12/what-separates-the-best-customers-from-the-merely-satisfied

https://3ccontactservices.com/ways-to-measure-emotion-in-customer-experience/

https://www.mindflash.com/blog/how-emotional-intelligence-training-improves-business-performance

https://chiefexecutive.net/how-an-emotional-connection-with-customers-is-helping-companies-win-the-battle-for-organic-growth/

https://thehustle.co/motivated-employees-can-increase-profits-by-almost-50-percent

http://www.motista.com/hubfs/Whitepapers/Motista%20FS%20White%20Paper.pdf

https://psychcentral.com/news/2016/01/14/emotional-tone-of-your-own-voice-affects-your-mood/97642.html

https://arxiv.org/ftp/arxiv/papers/1710/1710.10198.pdf

http://theladiescoach.com/business-and-money/tone-of-voice-misunderstood/

https://www.frontiersin.org/articles/10.3389/fnins.2016.00506/full

http://smallbusiness.chron.com/effects-poor-communication-business-345.html

http://globalbizresearch.org/economics/images/files/54946_ID_S528_JEIEFB_Maurice%20Odine.pdf

https://exploringyourmind.com/the-effects-of-distrust-in-our-relationships/

http://www.grapevinesurveys.com/blog/why-employee-loyalty-is-important

http://www.contractormag.com/columns/broudy/role-model-employees-0310

https://www.corporaterewards.co.uk/news-ideas/advantages-of-employee-retention/

http://smallbusiness.chron.com/effects-team-commitment-42028.html

http://smallbusiness.chron.com/effects-team-commitment-42028.html

https://explore.easyprojects.net/blog/5-ways-workplace-communication-effectiveness-can-increase-productivity

https://www.printwand.com/blog/importance-of-tone-in-business-writing-and-how-to-use-it

https://pilotonline.com/inside-business/news/columns/article_f69a71cb-fe33-589f-b9dc-07652c43be5e.html

https://www.businessworld.ie/news/10-Reasons-Why-Business-Writing-Skills-Are-So-Important-569924.html

https://www.entrepreneur.com/article/239330

http://www.customerexperienceinsight.com/7-writing-skills-to-please-customers/

https://open.lib.umn.edu/principlesmarketing/chapter/14-3-customer-satisfaction/

https://www.businessblogshub.com/2017/02/happy-customers-always-spend-more/

https://www.jstor.org/stable/30162046?seq=1#page_scan_tab_contents

https://fmoutsource.com/resources/how-customer-service-affects-sales/

http://www.iscsjournal.com/Makaleler/1731758883_3c4s_11.pdf

FROM THE AUTHOR

I would like to take this opportunity to thank all my readers for their time to read this book, which has taken me years of research, surveys and interview which had been useful and finally had the opportunity in publishing this book. To my publisher ***"Partridge Publishing Singapore"*** thank you for reaching out to me and making my dream come through by way of this book.

I would also like to dedicate this book to my family ***"Lt. Col (RTD) Datuk Dr. Senasi Annamalai*** "Consultant General Surgeon" (Father), ***Datin Padmani Devi Senasi*** (Mother), ***Menaga Devi Senasi*** (Sister), ***Dr. Ramdas Senasi*** "Paediatric Radiologist" (Elder brother) ***Vivasnathan Senasi*** (Brother), ***Sarvin Senasi Sharmadas*** (Son) and ***Neha Sonelli Devi*** (Daughter) for their countless support and patience in completing this book.

Finally I would like to dedicate this book and thank my former lecturer from Barry College in Wales, Cardiff ***"Miss Elizabeth***

Dyson Jones" for always believing in me, ***Mr Devia Nathan Ganapragasam*** from ***"Careers of Hospitality"*** for his support and my one and only good friend from Cardiff ***"Nick Tudor"*** who has always been motivating me ever since we were reconnected after several years.

Dr. Sharmadas Senasi has almost 20 years' experience of extensive ***Business Management, Hotel Management, Human Resource Development and Hospitality*** background in a multicultural environment in ***food and beverage services, hotel & resort operational management, business development, human behaviours, appraisals development management, leadership, SOP development, training, asset development, events management in banquet operations, menu constructions and human resources operations.***

He is backed with strong, decisive senior management leadership in organisations ranging from hotel start-up to developing a strong team. His management style is centred on impact-driven managerial skills and operations management in the hospitality industry. The strength which he has obtained through hard committeemen, training and developing has enabled him to complete his ***Hospitality Management in*** "Barry College" Wales – Cardiff, then continued with his ***Masters of Business Administration.*** He then pursued his **Doctorate in Business Administration** where his Dissertation Topic of **"Tonality in Communication between different ethnicity to improve customer satisfaction and increase profitability"** has been accepted successfully. Using these tools has made his decision making very meticulous, management skills which has been enhanced and allows him to train and develop his assets development in the hotel industry to be a key success.

The joy of training and guiding new recruits has been his biggest aspiration in a business environment.

This experience he has gathered in and around Malaysia and the United Kingdom has enriched his experience his work in Terengganu at ***"Pulau Perhentian, Redang and Lang Tengah",*** has widened his arena in managing and setting up a City Hotels and Resort. His forte in Food and Beverage Operations, Training and Development has enabled him to train, develop and to create great assets in the Hospitality Industry.

This was an outstanding journey for me in writing this book, a dream that has been delayed for a while and now it has become a reality. I am proud of this achievement I have set, a benchmark where I have concluded in my years in the Hospitality Industry.